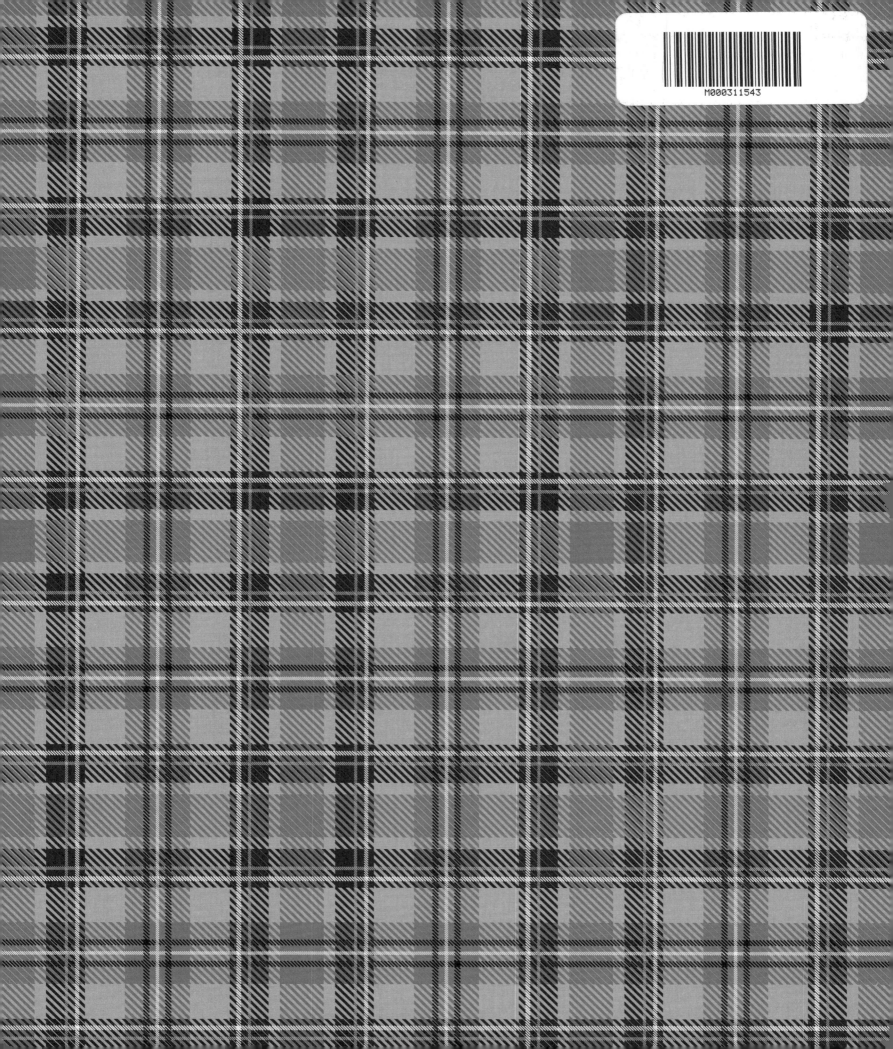

OUR FUTURE KING

PRINCE CHARLES AT 70

SJH Group
298 Regents Park Road, London N3 2SZ

www.sjhgroup.com

Printed in the UK by CPi Colour.
This paper has been independently certified according to
the standards of the Forest Stewardship Council® (FSC)®.

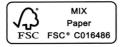

ISBN: 978-1-906670-71-9

Contents

Introduction 005

CHAPTER ONE
Born to be king: A celebrated arrival 012

CHAPTER TWO
Growing pains: School days and early life 020

CHAPTER THREE
Crowning of a prince: Charles's investiture ... 034

CHAPTER FOUR
The action man prince: Charles's military career ... 044

CHAPTER FIVE
In Charles we trust: The philanthropic prince ... 056

CHAPTER SIX
Husband and father: The Diana years 066

CHAPTER SEVEN
A fresh start: Charles and his new wife 076

CHAPTER EIGHT
Philosopher prince: Saving the planet 088

CHAPTER NINE
Commonwealth champion: The global ambassador ... 098

CHAPTER TEN
Shadow King: Monarch without a crown 108

CHAPTER ELEVEN
Ecological awareness: Caring for the environment ... 118
 A natural selection 120
 Sky Ocean Ventures 122
 Rare Breeds Survival Trust 126
 Brooke: Action for Working Horses and Donkeys ... 128

CHAPTER TWELVE
Sustainable fashion and fabrics: Smart materials ... 130

The fabric of life 132
The Woolmark Company 134
Harris Tweed Hebrides 136
Textile Exchange 138
Camira Fabrics 140

CHAPTER THIRTEEN
Captain of industry: Responsible business 142
 A wealth of ideas 144
 Tata Steel 146
 All Steels Trading Limited 148
 Minesoft 150
 Ceuta Group 152
 Al Habtoor Group 154

CHAPTER FOURTEEN
Iconic style: For the love of arts and crafts ... 156
 A cut above 158
 Curteis 160
 Rebecca Kellett 162
 Carolyn Lo 164
 Ivana Bags 166
 Kohinoor Jewellers 168
 Chilstone 170

CHAPTER FIFTEEN
Sustainable food: Connecting with the food chain ... 172
 From plough to plate 174
 Samworth Brothers 176
 A.E. Rodda & Son Limited 178
 Hildon Water 180
 Baxters Food Group 182
 McDonald's Corporation 184
 Bidfood 186
 Walkers Shortbread 188

CHAPTER SIXTEEN
Global hospitality: Entertaining in style 190
 Abroad appeal 192
 Lauren Berger Collection 194
 D1 London 196

Archaeological Paths 198
East Winds St Lucia 200
Reignwood Investments UK 202

CHAPTER SEVENTEEN
Leaders in learning: Education for everyone 204
The knowledge champion 206
Hornsey School for Girls 208
Ben-Gurion Univerity of the Negev 210
British International School of Wrocław 212
L'Ecole des Petits & L'Ecole de Battersea 214
University College School, Hampstead 216
Dragon School 218
Convent of Jesus and Mary Language College 220
Ark Boulton Academy 222
NOCN 224
Fourah Bay College, Sierra Leone 226
St John's University of Tanzania 228
Caribbean Maritime University 230
Canadian Nurses Association 232
Ghana International School 234

APPENDICES
Prince Charles's official titles 236

The Prince's coat of arms 238

About the publisher 239

Credits 240

Introduction

ROBERT JOBSON, ROYAL BIOGRAPHER

His Royal Highness Charles, Prince of Wales, is the heir apparent to the British throne as the eldest child of Queen Elizabeth II. He has been Duke of Cornwall and Duke of Rothesay since 1952. He was created Prince of Wales on 26 July 1958, six years after he became heir apparent, and had to wait another 11 years for his investiture, on 1 July 1969 at the medieval fortress of Caernarfon Castle, often anglicised as Carnarvon Castle, in Gwynedd, north-west Wales. At 70, on 14 November 2018, he is already the oldest and longest-serving heir apparent in British history.

His has not been a life spent waiting for the top job as monarch, but one devoted to public service, to supporting his mother the monarch, to helping put the "Great" back in Great Britain and promoting the realms, dominions and wider Commonwealth of which he has been named as its next head.

Charles is a serious, dedicated and deep-thinking man. A tireless campaigner who throughout his life of public service has devoted himself to promoting and protecting what is good about our country, the wider Commonwealth and its people. A trailblazing charitable entrepreneur, he established The Prince's Trust 42 years ago using his Royal Navy severance pay to help disadvantaged and vulnerable young people. It has been an inspiration and a lifeline to generations of young people.

The Prince has a ferocious appetite for work, carrying well over 500 of engagements in Britain and around the world every year. That workload has sought to meet a wide-range of challenges. Since 1976, the Prince's portfolio of charities grew to represent a broad range of areas including the built environment, the arts, responsible business and enterprise, young people, global sustainability and rural affairs. He was patron or president of more than 400 organisations. Incredibly, in the last decade alone the Prince's charities have raised more than £1 billion. For more than 30 years, he has been at the vanguard of a growing ecological movement.

Ahead of Charles's milestone 70th birthday this November Charles announced a major restructuring of his charities as he began planning for a future in which he will be king. The restructuring was to maximise the impact of his charities. "As I approach something of a milestone in my own life, I have had a chance to reflect. As I look at the results of the re-organisation, I have a strong sense of optimism and anticipation for what more may be achieved."

The changes mean a new and expanded Prince's Trust Group, to include the work of The Prince's Trust, continues to provide meaningful help to disadvantaged and vulnerable young people. In addition, in the forming of The Prince's Foundation, pulls together other strands of his charitable work.

After originally being treated with scepticism, many of Charles's pioneering ideas are now widely accepted and are gaining increasing impact. The Prince's passion for a more balanced, sustainable world — a human race living in harmony with nature — is central to his life's work. It is a responsibility he feels deeply about and all the more acutely now he is a grandfather.

But even before the births of Prince George, Princess Charlotte and Prince Louis, the Prince said publicly that he did not want to "hand on an increasingly dysfunctional world" to his grandchildren. He went on: "I don't want to be confronted by my future grandchild and them saying, 'Why didn't you do something?'"

"When he becomes King Charles III, he will be 'inspired' by the examples of his mother and his grandfather"

THE GREEN PRINCE

The invitation by French President Francois Hollande for Charles to deliver the keynote speech at the opening of the 21st Conference of the Parties (COP21) in November 2015 reflects the international recognition for his work on the environment.

He attended this United Nations Climate Change Conference alongside some 150 heads of state and also gave a keynote address on tropical forests and forest restoration on the Forests Day of the conference.

He has also been the driving force in a number of ground-breaking initiatives. In 2007 he launched the London-based Prince's Rainforests Project to try to help slow down the loss of the tropical rainforests. His work has also embraced the subject of fish stocks and how best to safeguard their future and the fishing industries they sustain. The work of the Prince's International Sustainability Unit (ISU) has resulted in more consensus between industry interests, non-governmental groups, scientists and governments on the need for new ways to invest in the future of fish stocks.

He has been active in drawing attention to the benefits of action on climate change, including for public health. A meeting convened by the ISU in 2015 made a clear link between cutting carbon emissions and improving the air we breathe.

The Prince has continued to draw attention to the importance of new buildings being in harmony with their natural surroundings.

He has highlighted what he sees as the vital relationship between cities and the countryside, particularly when it comes to a sustainable food supply.

In 1986 Charles set up the Prince's Foundation for Building Community (PFBC) – initially known as The Prince of Wales's Institution of Architecture – in the belief that sustainably planned, built and maintained communities improve the quality of life of everyone who's part of them. He argues that neighbourhoods thrive when developers, architects and craftsmen work in partnership with those who live and work there. All these initiatives will ensure the Prince — as heir to the throne — has left his mark.

The Prince is fully aware that he will have to make adjustments if fate calls upon him to become king, according to those close to him. Should that moment come he will, of course, fully accept and embrace his duty. Equally, he understands too the "limitations" that being Sovereign brings.

Those close to him say that when he becomes King Charles III, he will be "inspired" by the examples of his mother, our longest reigning monarch, and his grandfather George VI, who died at 56. But, whether short or long, it is clear that Charles will define his reign himself. This will be "his" reign, his way. He will draw on a lifetime of public service in shaping that reign, which does not have to be in any way a carbon copy of his mother's.

Charles has always encouraged issues that, without his support, might otherwise receive little exposure. For instance, he and promoted tolerance and greater understanding between different faiths and communities.

Opposite: *The Queen presents Prince Charles with the Royal Horticultural Society's Victoria Medal of Honour, May 2009*

Opposite: *The Prince speaking during the opening ceremony of the United Nations Climate Change Conference in Copenhagen, December 2009*

Above: *Charles attends a reception in Manchester Town Hall following the Manchester Arena bombing, June 2017*

A loving husband, father and grandfather, Charles is undoubtedly a visionary. He is a man whose sensitive, responsive nature too means he will always have the good of his future subjects sincerely at heart. Never afraid to step into a controversial debate, he took centre-stage over London's housing crisis in 2014, warning that soaring prices would drive a generation of young people away.

When asked what would happen to his charities, Prince Charles has been clear: "Well, if we would have any chance of anything continuing, then you have to endow the main ones, somehow." But whatever happens going forward, the Prince has left his mark on Britain and the wider Commonwealth.

As the UK defines new types of partnership with our friends inside and outside the European Union, the Prince, supported ably by his wife The Duchess of Cornwall, continues to work hard – at home and abroad – to protect and enhance the UK's interests. The Prince arrived in Romania on the day that the UK government triggered Article 50 of the EU Lisbon Treaty, beginning the process for leaving the EU. The visit was a valuable opportunity to celebrate with the people of Romania, and subsequently in Italy and Austria, some of the many aspects of the friendship between our peoples; a friendship that will endure.

A WORKING ROYAL

The retirement of The Duke of Edinburgh is already seeing all members of the Royal Family helping to fill the considerable gap that the well-earned easing of Prince Philip's incredible workload brought. At the State Opening of Parliament, the Prince of Wales offered exactly this support to the Queen.

The sheer scope and diversity of duties, ranging from the sort of State occasions that people often say, "make us proud to be British", through to work to support our military, not to mention communities of every faith and none, and of every ethnic origin, helps to bind us all together as a single, united kingdom.

In the past year the Prince has visited 10 Commonwealth countries. In April 2018 he hosted the formal opening in London of the latest Commonwealth Heads of Government Meeting, or CHOGM as it is known. That was a hugely successful event, with the UK Prime Minister receiving the baton as incoming Chair. The summit decided unanimously that The Prince of Wales should succeed the Queen as Head of The Commonwealth, in the fullness of time.

Closer to home, the year was also punctuated by tragic incidents, including terrorist atrocities in London and Manchester and, of course, the heartbreaking fire at Grenfell Tower in west London. In the wake of these events, both Charles and Camilla visited those who had been affected together with members of the police, emergency services and medical teams who were involved in these difficult moments and whose brave work they wanted to recognise personally.

"This milestone birthday gives us the chance not only to praise His Royal Highness but also to celebrate his achievements"

Prince Charles has also been vocal on the issues of religious tolerance and greater cultural cohesion. These were the focus an Easter message that was broadcast globally on Good Friday, reaching a global audience of more than 10 million.

In contrast to these sombre events, the year was also punctuated with moments of great joy within The Royal Family. Prince Harry and Meghan Markle – now the Duke and Duchess of Sussex – were engaged in November 2017. Their wedding on 19 May 2018 seemed like a day when it was not just the sun that shone, but Britain itself radiated, right around the world. The Duke and Duchess of Cambridge announced they were expecting another child and the Prince of Wales's third grandchild, Prince Louis, was born in April. The Duchess of Cornwall celebrated her 70th birthday. The Prince of Wales is catching her up and of course celebrates his own 70th birthday in November this year.

As a public servant he represents good value for money. The taxpayer meets less than 10 per cent of the total costs for the Prince and the Duchess of Cornwall who are funded by his landed estate, the Duchy of Cornwall.

As a royal correspondent of more than 25 years experience, I have travelled the world alongside the Prince. I have chatted with him, interviewed him and written a biography about him. I have witnessed too what a diligent and deeply caring man he is, determined to do his best for the greater good of humanity and nature.

This milestone birthday gives us the chance not only to praise His Royal Highness but also to celebrate his life and his many laudable achievements. Privately, modestly, he gives the impression he feels vindicated in his years of campaigning over issues such as agriculture, the environment and architecture that matter so much to him. He certainly shows no signs of slowing down after a lifetime of pioneering – quite the opposite. "If you stick to your guns," he once said to the *Financial Times*, "sometimes years later you suddenly find that some of these things are starting to appeal to people."

And, without doubt, the Prince has certainly stuck to his guns.

Camilla, Charles, William and Harry pictured during The Prince's Trust 30th Birthday Concert at the Tower of London, May 2006

CHAPTER ONE

Born to be king
A celebrated arrival

The news of Charles's birth was heralded with great cheer across the British Empire, but little more than three years on, the young prince would find himself heir to the throne, following the death of his grandfather King George VI

The distinctive voice of BBC presentation, director John Snagge, crackled onto the radio, just as it had done when he delivered important radio announcements throughout the Second World War, with a late-night news item. It was 14 November 1948.

"This is the BBC Home Service," he announced, in his familiar cut-glass tones. "It has just been announced from Buckingham Palace that Her Royal Highness Princess Elizabeth, Duchess of Edinburgh, was safely delivered of a prince at 9.14pm and that Her Royal Highness and her son are both doing well. Listeners will wish us to offer their royal congratulations to Princess Elizabeth and the Royal Family on this happy occasion." Patriotically, the national anthem was then played across the airwaves in honour of the as yet unnamed baby prince.

The British Empire may have been in irreversible decline by this stage, but the public's respect for the institution embodied by the baby's grandfather, George VI, and his family had never been stronger. The Countess Granville, the infant's great aunt, could not contain her excitement when she first saw the little prince. "He could not be more angelic looking," she said. "He is golden-haired and has the most beautiful complexion, as well as amazingly delicate features for so young a baby."

Princess Elizabeth, then just 22, was less glowing about her first baby. For some reason she fixated on his hands: "Rather large but fine with long fingers," said the future Queen, "quite unlike mine and certainly not like his father's. It will be interesting to see what they become."

A JOYOUS OCCASION

The news of Prince Charles's birth sparked celebrations throughout the British Empire. An editorial in *The Times* newspaper described King George VI as the nation's "supreme representative", which "in modern times is a more royal function than any duty of state," affirming that, "the representative monarchy has made every one of its subjects feel friend and neighbour to the Royal Family; and so it is that the simple joy which the coming of this child has brought to them is shared by all."

A few weeks later, on the 15 December 1948, the baby prince, second in line to the British throne, was baptised Charles Philip Arthur George in the Music Room at Buckingham Palace. The then Archbishop of Canterbury, Geoffrey Fisher, presided over the ceremony and used water from the River Jordan to anoint the baby's head. Pathé News reels showed the public footage of Princess Elizabeth holding Charles in her arms, sat alongside her mother,

Above: *Princess Elizabeth and Prince Philip with a young Prince Charles, July 1949*

Opposite: *Prince Charles and his mother play hide and seek, October 1950*

"The King marked Charles's third birthday with a photograph of them together – one of the Prince's abiding memories of his grandfather"

Above: *King George VI and Queen Elizabeth with Prince Charles and Princess Anne, photographed on Charles's third birthday, November 1951*

Queen Elizabeth, then 48, and grandmother Queen Mary, 81, consort to the late King George V.

Baby Charles wore a baptism gown first used by Queen Victoria's first born in 1841, an intricate satin-and-lace robe, as he was admitted to the Church of England.

The new parents moved out of their Buckingham Palace apartment a few hundred yards away down The Mall to the newly refurbished Clarence House. Two nannies, Helen Lightbody and Mabel Anderson, took charge of the royal nursery. In addition, Charles was watched over around the clock by Metropolitan Police officers. It was something he would have to get used to.

Charles's father, Prince Philip, was still a serving officer in the Royal Navy, while Princess Elizabeth was increasingly occupied with her role as heiress-presumptive and supporting her father, who was in frail health. Effectively, it meant the royal nannies took charge of the daily care of Charles – although Princess Elizabeth made sure whenever possible to attend bath time and would stay to read her son a bedtime story.

In August 1950, Princess Anne was born and joined her brother in the nursery. By now, however, the heavy burden of public duty meant Princess Elizabeth could not spend as much time with her young children as she would have wanted.

The King's health was in rapid decline and she had to step in to public engagements that he was not up to. Elizabeth knew too that she had to start preparing herself for the role as monarch. It may have been unspoken but she knew her father was dying.

Within days of Charles's second birthday, the Queen joined her husband in Malta without the children. Philip had just been promoted to the rank of Commander of a Royal Navy frigate, and his career was going from strength to strength. Charles and the four-month-old Anne remained at home in the care of their grandparents and nannies.

At the time the King, gravely ill, was recuperating from the last of three operations. He celebrated Charles's third birthday and marked it with a photograph of them together. Charles would later admit that this special shared photograph was one of his abiding personal memories of his grandfather.

A month later the family was reunited for Christmas. Days later, the King waved his daughter off on a Commonwealth tour that he had been forced to postpone four years previously. The crowd gave the King a sympathetic cheer as he stood in the bitter cold to wave goodbye as his beloved daughter left for Africa. He gave his customary wave of acknowledgement and then turned to Margaret "Bobo" MacDonald, Princess Elizabeth's loyal assistant. "Look after the princess for me,"

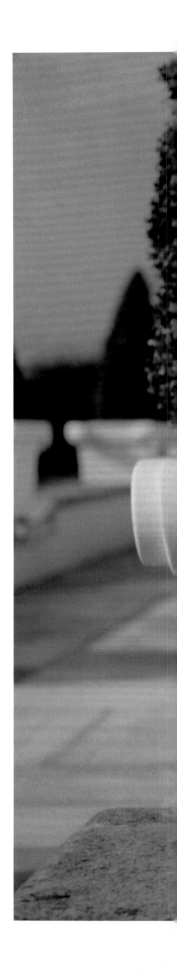

said the King. Margaret MacDonald later admitted that she had never seen the King so upset.

Elizabeth was not to see her father alive again. Six days after they had said goodbye, in the early hours of 6 February 1952, George VI died in his sleep of thrombosis at his Sandringham estate in Norfolk. He was only 56 years old and had reigned for just 16 years.

A NEW MONARCH

Buckingham Palace officials held up the announcement of the monarch's passing for three hours while they desperately attempted to contact Elizabeth. Oblivious, the royal couple had just returned from the Treetops hotel and observation tower to Sagana Lodge in Kenya. They could not be reached.

A telegram sent to Government House in Nairobi could not be decoded because the keys to the safe holding the codebook were unavailable. Meanwhile, "Operation Hyde Park Corner" – the code name for arrangements for the death of the King – was well underway. But Elizabeth still did not know that she was already Queen.

Prime Minister Winston Churchill had been informed of the King's death. When his staff tried to console him, saying he would get on well with the new Queen, Churchill replied that he barely knew her and she was "only a child".

The widowed Queen Elizabeth set out her thoughts in a letter to Queen Mary, in which she worried about the burden that would fall on the 25-year-old Elizabeth. "My darling Mama, what can I say to you – I know that you loved Bertie dearly, and he was my whole life, and one can only be deeply thankful for the utterly happy years we had together. He was so wonderfully thoughtful and loving, and I don't believe he ever thought of himself at all ... I cannot bear to think of Lilibet, so young to bear such a burden – I do feel for you so darling Mama – to lose two dear sons, and Bertie still so young and so precious – it is almost more than one can bear, your very loving Elizabeth."

Elizabeth was now Queen. Charles, at just three years old, a sensitive and somewhat shy boy, was given the title The Duke of Cornwall upon his grandfather's death. He was now the direct heir to the throne.

Queen Elizabeth pictured
with her grandson Prince
Charles and Pippin the dog

Opposite: *The Queen and
Prince Philip with their two
young children at Balmoral
Castle, September 1952*

CHAPTER TWO

Growing pains
School days and early life

From nursery classroom to boarding school to the hallowed halls of Cambridge, Prince Charles's education was one of personal trials and triumphs lived out in the public spotlight

A little over a year after the death of his grandfather King George VI, the four-year-old Charles attended his mother's magnificent coronation at Westminster Abbey – the first to be televised. Afterwards he was brought out on to the palace balcony as Her Majesty acknowledged the cheers of the huge and enthusiastic crowd below. By now the Prince was starting to comprehend that his life was very different to that of other children.

More than 8,000 guests attended Queen Elizabeth II's coronation. When she took the Coronation Oath, binding her to serve the people and maintain the laws of God, millions around the world tuned in to witness the historic moment. Some had bought television sets – then a rarity in Britain and much of the world – purely for this occasion. Perhaps, this glamorous new Queen was just what the war-weary British people needed. The image of the youthful Elizabeth with the heavy crown on her head was one the most iconic photographs of the age.

Within months she was handed a colossal diplomatic mission — to lead the transformation from British Empire to Commonwealth over a marathon six-month tour, to cement her position as symbolic leader of much of the free world. It was her chance to stamp her personality on the Commonwealth. It meant her young children would be left without their parents again as the Queen toured 13 countries in the West Indies, Australasia, Asia and Africa, covering a staggering 43,618 miles. Many of the countries had never before seen their monarch. It included 10,000 miles by plane, 2,000 miles by car, 2,500 by rail and the rest by sea, most of it on board the Royal Yacht SS *The Gothic*. The final leg home was on the newly commissioned Royal Yacht *Britannia*.

When the Queen and Prince Philip completed their final leg home on the new Royal Yacht, from Tobruk on the north African coast, Charles and Anne were waiting patiently for them. Her Majesty later joked: "They were extremely polite. I don't think they knew who we were at all!" The Queen was their mother and her dedication to duty was something that the two children would have to endure.

Shortly before Charles's fifth birthday, one of the rooms of the nursery was converted to a classroom and Catherine Peebles was engaged as a governess to teach the heir to the throne some primary-school skills. Peebles – who had previously worked with the Baroness d'Arcy de Knayth and the Duchess of Kent's children – soon discovered that the way to get the best out of the young Charles was to be encouraging. He excelled at drawing and also enjoyed singing. The Prince's affectionate nickname for Peebles was "Mipsy".

On 14 April 1954, Prince Charles and his sister, Anne, boarded the Royal Yacht *Britannia* bound for Malta, in order to join their parents for the official visit there before continuing on to Gibraltar, their first official foreign visit. Charles took his sister's hand as she patted down the steps, shepherded her carefully into the car, and turned to wave to the press.

SCHOOL DAYS

Just before his eighth birthday Charles broke with the royal tradition of being home-schooled and joined the pre-preparatory school Hill House in Knightsbridge, west London. The Prince got to play sports with other boys and even travelled on public transport. He mixed with the other pupils and made reasonable progress as a student. Away from

Below: *The Prince plays in his toy car at Balmoral while his mother looks on, September 1952*

"The rough and tumble of boarding school shook him into action and the Prince taught himself to wrestle and box"

Opposite: *Cheam schoolboy Charles, aged 10, pictured the day after being created the Prince of Wales*

school his father, Prince Philip, was determined to introduce his son to the adventure of rural life. He taught his son to fish and shoot but the Duke's blunt manner and attempts to mould the boy into his idea of a son to be proud of stifled their relationship.

In September 1957 the Prince had to face a new challenge when he was sent to Cheam School in Surrey. Founded in the 17th century, this boarding school housed around 80 boys between the ages of eight and 14. Prince Philip, a former Cheam pupil himself, felt the school had helped to toughen his character and wanted the same for his son.

Headmaster Peter Beck said that, while the school was honoured to have the Prince as a pupil, he would be treated the same as any other boy. His parents dropped him off, amid a media frenzy, and stayed long enough to see where Charles would sleep, but then left. At first Charles struggled with homesickness and found it difficult to mix. "It was not easy to make large numbers of friends," he recalled, many years later. "I'm not a gregarious person so I've always had a horror of gangs ... I have always preferred my own company or just a one-to-one."

The rough and tumble of boarding shook him into action and, quite wisely, the Prince taught himself to wrestle and box. He was, as a result, able take care of himself in a playground fight, although it did result in the future king receiving corporal punishment, which he later admitted worked for him. "I didn't do it again," he said.

In summer term of 1958, headmaster Beck summoned Charles and a group of boys to his study. It was the last day of the Empire and Commonwealth Games in Cardiff and the boys were allowed to watch the closing ceremony on his television. The Queen was unable to attend in person due to an attack of

sinusitis, but a pre-recorded message was played. She appeared on the screen with a simple message: "The British Empire and Commonwealth Games in the capital... have made this a memorable year for the Principality. I have therefore decided to mark it further by an act which will, I hope, give much pleasure to all Welshmen as it does to me. I intend to create my son Charles, Prince of Wales today ... When he is grown up, I will present him to you at Caernarfon."

He had now become His Royal Highness Prince Charles Philip Arthur George, Prince of Wales and Earl of Chester, Duke of Cornwall, Duke of Rothesay, Earl of Carrick, Lord of the Isles and Baron of Renfrew and Great Steward of Scotland. His school friends all congratulated him. The newspapers too were enthusiastic about the decision.

Two weeks' later, the Royal Family visited Anglesey in the Royal Yacht en route for Scotland. Once ashore, the Prince was greeted with great enthusiasm. The Principality had a new prince, and it was clearly delighted. Cheering crowds broke through the police cordons. An excited dog nearly knocked the heir to the throne to the ground. The Prince kept his composure and patted the dog. Prince Philip put a reassuring arm around his son's shoulder in an act of paternal care and both father and son waved to the crowd.

In 1962, after five years at Cheam, he was made head boy. Although he was later to say he loathed his time there, it had certainly helped him develop as a person. He was academically competent, had discovered a love for acting and also captained the school's first eleven at football, played in the first eleven at cricket and in the first fifteen at rugby.

Where the future king should be educated next became a source of constant speculation. Eton College was the popular

"Charles started to enjoy school life without being stricken by fearful bouts of homesickness. His letters told of what he was doing rather than expressing the bitter pain of missing his family"

Opposite: *The Prince arrives for his first term at Gordonstoun School, accompanied by his father and Captain Iain Tennant of the school's board of governors, May 1962*

Right: *Charles is shown around his new school by Captain Iain Tennant*

choice, favoured too by the Queen Mother, but Prince Philip had other ideas. The Queen left the decision to her husband and his choice was his old school boarding Gordonstoun.

COLDITZ WITH KILTS

Established in 1934 on the shores of the Moray Firth in north-east Scotland, Gordonstoun was the brainchild of headmaster Dr Kurt Hahn, a refugee from Nazi Germany who was inspired by Plato. He believed that good and wise government can only occur when philosophers become rulers or rulers become philosophers. This could only be achieved through education: not just through academic education, he believed, but also moral and physical training of the mind, the body and in particular the character.

Charles was delivered into this spartan world by his father and allocated to Windmill Lodge, one of seven houses scattered through the grounds. Like the other houses, Windmill Lodge was a wooden hut that had been acquired from the Royal Air Force as temporary accommodation years before, but never replaced. At night the windows were kept open by order, even if the weather was poor, which it often was. If a student was unlucky enough to have been allocated a bed near to one of these windows, as Charles was, he would invariably awake to a rain-soaked bed in spring, summer or autumn, or one covered in snow in the winter.

Charles arrived as Hahn had retired and had been replaced by Robert Chew. A warning was sent out to other boys that anyone caught bullying the heir to the throne risked immediate expulsion. This had the opposite effect. Charles was picked upon at once, "maliciously, cruelly and without respite".

The Prince took this thuggery without complaint. But he was in private despair. "I hate coming back here and leaving everyone at home," he wrote in one of his letters home. "I hardly get any sleep at the House because I snore and get hit on the head the whole time. It is absolute hell."

For Prince Philip his time at Gordonstoun had been an edifying and character-building experience. But, as the school tottered into the swinging sixties, many of the students were a law unto themselves, and Charles found himself at the receiving end of some brutal treatment from his peers. "A prison sentence," was how Charles later described it. "It's Colditz with kilts."

One infamous event unfolded while he was a pupil, which made headline news. Charles developed his sailing skills and in his second year, he joined the crew of *Pinta*, one of two ketches owned by the school. On his first trip in the summer of 1963, he sailed into Stornoway Harbour on the Isle of Lewis. He and four other boys were given shore leave to have dinner and then see a film. Charles was accompanied by the Prince's policeman, Donald Green. As they walked towards the

A smiling Prince Charles shakes hands with a group of school children during a royal visit in Australia, May 1966

"The Prince did not look forward to returning to Gordonstoun but his stay in Australia had given him newfound confidence"

Crown Hotel they began to attract a small crowd. By the time they were in the lounge a larger crowd had gathered outside the main window and flash bulbs were going off as folk jostled to get a photograph. Embarrassed by all the attention, Charles retreated from the room and, followed by his detective, found himself in the public bar.

"Everybody was looking at me. And I thought, I must have a drink – that's what you are supposed to do in a bar. I went and sat down at the bar and the barman said, 'What do you want to drink?' I thought that you had to have alcohol in a bar, so I said, 'Cherry brandy'." At that very moment a female journalist walked into the bar and so the incident was to become headline news.

At first, the Palace denied the story was true. But it wouldn't go away. Two days later the Palace was forced to withdraw its denial with press secretary Richard Colville claiming that he had been initially misled by the Prince's detective and so he sincerely regretted giving the newspapers incorrect information. The consequences of this were serious for both the Prince and Donald Green. Once back at school, Charles was sent for by the headmaster and was demoted a rank in the school system. Green was unfairly removed from royal duties, which horrified the Prince.

QUITE THE PERFORMER

In 1964 teacher Eric Anderson, who in later life would become headmaster of Eton, set about putting on a production Shakespeare's *Henry V* and asked for volunteer actors. Charles applied and proved to be a fine character actor, however,

Anderson didn't cast him in the lead role. Instead he gave the young Prince the part of Exeter. The play was a success, but the audience of local people insisted that it was a pity Charles, the best actor, didn't play Henry.

Encouraged by this, Anderson persuaded the headmaster that there should be a winter play as well. In November, a production of *Macbeth* was hastily planned and the Prince of Wales was offered the title role. His performance was sensitive, regal and convincing and amazed the producer, the staff, the pupils and even his father, who came to watch.

Charles was sent to Timbertop in Australia to help with his development. At first the Prince feared the worst but, to his amazement, he found the boys and masters friendly, and got on very well with his room-mate. More importantly, Timbertop was what Gordonstoun had been when his father had attended. As a result, for the first time, Charles started to enjoy school life without being stricken by fearful bouts of homesickness. His letters told of what he was doing rather than expressing the bitter pain of missing his family.

In between his outdoor adventures of long walks and climbing, Charles was expected to teach himself A-level French and History. This he did, but he often found it more congenial to go trout fishing in a nearby stream. Prince Charles left Australia with sadness. In a statement he thanked the Australian people for "a marvellous and worthwhile experience" and for their kindness, adding that he was very sorry to be leaving. He meant it. He has loved visiting Australia ever since.

The Prince did not look forward to returning to Gordonstoun but he was now approaching 18 and his stay in Australia had given him newfound confidence. To his surprise he was appointed head boy, an appointment that gave him the opportunity to start to reform the brutal Gordonstoun society and banish its bullying culture.

In July 1967, Prince Charles became the first heir to the throne openly to test his own academic ability by sitting his A-level examinations for university. He received a commendable grade B in History and a satisfactory grade C in French. He also took a special paper in History, designed for high-flyers to test their judgement, initiative and acumen. According to the secretary of the examining board, he had shone.

It was decided that the Prince should attend university first and then serve in one or more of the armed forces. But which university? After nine months of discussion it was eventually decided to go for Trinity College Cambridge. Charles decided to read anthropology and archaeology and wanted to do so via a standard, full, three-year tripos, and would thus be judged entirely on his own abilities.

UNIVERSITY CHALLENGE

He arrived at university and buckled down to his studies, conscious that his results would be subject to the scrutiny of the press. After four terms at Trinity, the Prince was sent to the University College of Wales at Aberystwyth in order to learn Welsh before his formal investiture as Prince of Wales. This was very much a political decision: in the late 1960s, a wave of nationalism was on the rise in Scotland and Wales.

More seriously, fanatics calling themselves the Free Wales Army were causing police and security services concern.

Upon his arrival at Pantycelyn Hall, where he was to share accommodation with 250 other students, he encountered a crowd of some 500 cheering locals. His experienced an incident-free spell at the university. At the end of his eight-week term he was invited to close the Urdd National Eisteddfod, the annual Welsh youth festival for poetry, drama and music, before an audience of some 6,000 people all crammed into a large marquee where he would make his first public speech of any significance in Welsh, a language that he had studied for just two months.

As he got to his feet demonstrators screamed abuse at the Prince. He stood his ground and just stared back at them without displaying any other emotion. The natural sympathy of the rest of the 6,000–strong audience was aroused and mayhem broke out. The end of his speech was greeted by a roar of approval and a standing ovation. "It was extraordinarily warming to have so many people applauding and cheering and as a result my nerves were dissipated by the time that I was allowed to get anywhere near the microphone," he noted later.

By May the Prince was back at the University of Cambridge to face the moment of truth with his history finals and was awarded a lower second-class degree, which, given all the disruption to his studies through royals duties, was deemed as a major achievement by the college and this was echoed by the national press. The Prince finished his academic education full of self-confidence. At times it had been a testing journey, but his strength of character had seen him through.

Above: *The Prince of Wales in his room at Trinity College, Cambridge, 1969*

Opposite: *Charles pictured during his time as an undergraduate at the University of Cambridge*

CHAPTER THREE

Crowning of a prince
Charles's investiture

Charles's investiture at Caernarfon in July 1969 saw the Prince of Wales cultivate strong links with the principality; links that have only grown deeper and more resolute over the intervening years

On 26 July 1958 the headmaster of Prince Charles's preparatory school at Cheam, Peter Beck, asked a small number of pupils to join him in his sitting room. The Prince was among them. The Commonwealth Games in Cardiff were being broadcast on the BBC and the boys were allowed to watch the closing ceremony on his television. It was announced that, while Her Majesty the Queen was not in attendance, she would address the stadium and the television audience in a recorded message. Her Majesty then appeared on the screen and read out a message that would have huge implications for the young Prince.

"The British Empire and Commonwealth Games in the capital… have made this a memorable year for the principality," announced the Queen. "I have therefore decided to mark it further by an act that will, I hope, give much pleasure to all Welshmen as it does to me. I intend to create my son Charles Prince of Wales today… When he is grown up, I will present him to you at Caernarfon."

Charles's friends turned and congratulated him on his elevation in status, which made the Prince a touch uncomfortable as he hated being the centre of attention.

At a dinner in Caerphilly Castle in July 2008 to celebrate his half-century as the Prince of Wales, Charles spoke of the moment. "I remember with horror and embarrassment how I was summoned with all the other boys at my school to the headmaster's sitting room, where we all had to sit on the floor and watch television," he said. "To my total embarrassment I heard my mama's voice – she wasn't very well at the time and could not go. My father went instead and a recording of the

message was played in the stadium saying that I was to be made the Prince of Wales. All the other boys turned around and looked at me and I remember thinking, 'What on earth have I been let in for?' That is my overriding memory."

The Prince said later it was one of the greatest privileges possible to be the 21st Prince of Wales. "I have tried my best," he said. "It may not be very adequate to live up to the motto of my predecessors, 'Ich Dien – I Serve'."

Eleven years after the Queen's announcement – on 1 July 1969 – he was sworn in as the Prince of Wales in an investiture at Caernarfon Castle, in a ceremony based on the one for his great-uncle David in 1911.

On the eve of the initiation the Prince joined the Queen and Prince Philip aboard the royal train and headed for North Wales. All three of them believed that it was essential this royal pageant had to go to plan and were eager for a positive reaction from the public, especially in Wales.

PREPARING FOR WALES

After completing four terms at Trinity College, Cambridge, the Prince was sent to the University College of Wales at Aberystwyth in order to learn Welsh before his formal investiture as the Prince of Wales. This was a political decision rather than a cultural one, amid a revival of nationalism in Scotland and Wales. Prior to his departure to the Welsh college, Charles recorded his first radio interview and, not surprisingly, he was asked about his attitude towards the hostility in the principality. "It would be unnatural, I think, if one didn't feel any apprehension about it," he said. "One always wonders

Above: *Her Majesty The Queen places the coronet of the Prince of Wales on Charles's head, July 1969*

Prince Charles descends the steps of Caernarvon Castle following his investiture as the Prince of Wales

"As long as I don't get covered in too much egg and tomato I'll be alright"

what's going to happen... As long as I don't get covered in too much egg and tomato I'll be alright. But I don't blame people demonstrating like that. They've never seen me before. They don't know what I'm like. I've hardly been to Wales, and you can't really expect people to be overzealous about the fact of having a so-called English prince to come amongst them."

To cancel the university term in Wales would have been a public-relations disaster for the government and indeed for Charles himself. It was decided it would be a weakness to bow to extremist threats. So they went ahead regardless. Upon his arrival at Pantycelyn Hall, where he would share accommodation with 250 other students, Charles was met by a 500-strong cheering crowd. The welcome raised his spirits. In the end the Prince enjoyed his time there and was treated kindly in Aberystwyth. His period of study there passed without incident.

He wrote to a friend: "If I have learned anything during the last eight weeks, it's been about Wales... they feel so strongly about Wales as a nation, and it means something to them, and they are depressed by what might happen to it if they don't try and preserve the language and the culture, which is unique and special to Wales, and if something is unique and special, I see it as well worth preserving."

Many years later the Prince recalled that the time he spent studying in Wales was among his fondest memories. "Memorable times spent exploring mid-Wales during my term at Aberystwyth University," he said with pleasure, "and learning something about the principality and its ancient language, folklore, myths and history."

PARAMILITARY THREATS

Despite this preparation in fealty to Charles's status within the Principality, more radical factions within the Welsh nationalist movement had started a disturbing campaign of terrorism. Fanatics had formed what they called the Free Wales Army and had finally gained the attention of the police and security services after an RAF warrant officer was seriously injured in an incident. The gang then planted a bomb that destroyed the Temple of Peace in Cardiff. Another bomb was found in the lost-luggage department of the railway station.

On the eve of the investiture, on 30 June, two members of a paramilitary organisation called Mudiad Amddiffyn Cymru (MAC – Movement for the Defence of Wales) were killed while placing a bomb outside government offices in the North Wales coastal town of Abergele. On the day of the investiture, two other bombs were planted in Caernarfon, one in the local police constable's garden which exploded as the 21-gun salute was fired. Another was planted in an iron forge near the castle but failed to go off. A final bomb was placed on the Llandudno Pier and was designed to stop the Royal Yacht Britannia from docking – this too failed to explode.

Anonymously, too, it was announced that the Prince of Wales was on their target list. This threat left Charles understandably concerned. The Royal Family was powerless in this regard and had to trust in the competency of the security services and the measures the police had already put in place to ensure the safety of both Charles and Her Majesty.

"Charles was paraded through the streets before retiring aboard the Royal Yacht at Holyhead, an emotionally exhausted but very happy prince"

Opposite and right: The Queen presents the Prince of Wales to the attending crowd

A WARM WELCOME

Thankfully, the streets of Caernarfon were peaceful during Charles's instalment as the Prince of Wales, on 1 July 1969. Charles was driven through the town in an open carriage on his way to the castle past cheering crowds. As the guests and choir sang "God Bless the Prince of Wales", he was conducted to the dais and knelt before the Queen. He would later write that he found it profoundly moving when he placed his hands between his mother's and spoke the oath of allegiance.

Her Majesty then presented the Prince to the crowd at Eagle Gate and at the lower ward to the sound of magnificent fanfares. After that he was again paraded through the streets before retiring aboard the Royal Yacht at Holyhead for a well-deserved dinner, an emotionally exhausted but very happy prince. Buoyed by the experience, the Prince noted, "As long as I do not take myself too seriously I should not be too badly off."

The next day the Prince embarked on a week of solo engagements around the principality. He recalled being "utterly amazed" by the positive reaction he received. As the tour progressed south, the crowds grew even bigger. At the end of it Charles arrived exhausted but elated at Windsor Castle. He retired to write up his diary, noting the silence after the day's cheers and applause and reflecting that he had much to live up to and hoped that he could do something constructive for Wales.

Since then, perhaps like no other bearer of the title, the Prince has cultivated close contacts within the principality.

He purchased a 192-acre estate near the village of Myddfai to the south of Llandovery in Carmarthenshire, through his Duchy of Cornwall trust, called Llwynywermod (also known as Llwynywormwood). Adapted from a former model farm and located just outside the Brecon Beacons National Park, it bears witness to Charles's philosophy of sustainable building with a structure traditionally made from existing and locally sourced materials, an ecologically sound heating system and elegant interiors that harmonise perfectly with the architecture.

He uses it for meetings, receptions and concerts, and as the base for his several yearly visits to Wales, including the annual week of summer engagements, known in his annual schedule as "Wales Week". Charles says he wants it to be "a showcase for traditional Welsh craftsmanship, textiles and woodwork, so as to draw attention to the high-quality small enterprises, woollen mills, quilt-makers, joiners, stonemasons and metalworkers situated in rural parts of Wales". It enables him, he says, to feel part of the local community. To him, he says, preserving this sense of community "is timeless".

During a January 2015 interview with Visit Wales, Charles was asked how important it was for him to have a retreat in Wales. "Very important!" he replied. "Having been Prince of Wales for 55 years [at the time of the interview], it enables me, on various occasions, to be part of the local community around Llandovery and to have a base for entertaining and meeting people from throughout the principality."

CHAPTER FOUR

The action man prince
Charles's military career

As a young man Charles followed his father into the Armed Forces – first the Royal Air Force and then the Royal Navy – before meeting someone who would play a huge role in his future life

Prince Philip had to pass up a most promising naval career due to his marriage to the heir to the throne, Princess Elizabeth. It's possibly why Philip was so keen to see his eldest son follow in his footsteps and embark upon a career in the Royal Navy. Officially Charles would sign up for three years, but it was expected he would stay for at least five so that he could not gain command of his own ship.

Charles was to enter the Royal Navy College, Dartmouth in autumn 1971 but before that it was decided that he should undertake an intensive four-month attachment to the Royal Air Force at Cranwell to gain his wings as a jet pilot. It was to be the start of the "action man" image that the media was determined to create about him. He flew to the college at RAF Cranwell in March 1971 at the controls of a twin-engine aircraft from the Queen's flight.

THE FLYING PRINCE

Two aircraft were assigned to the Prince for his use only. They were separated from the others and maintained only by a special team and guarded by RAF police. While Charles was allowed to undertake the course, anything that involved any high-risk elements was ruled out.

The Prince loved his time at Cranwell and penned letters to Lord Mountbatten in which he enthused about the lectures on jet engines. "To my amazement I find I am beginning to understand some of it and I am convinced that the secret is continuity all day every day," he wrote. "They certainly keep you busy here and I am up early and in bed fairly early as well."

After just two weeks of ground training he was allowed to take the controls of a Jet Provost and, while he found navigation

tricky he was soon permitted to make his first solo flight on 31 March 1971, just three weeks after arriving at Cranwell. "I did one circuit and managed to bring off a very passable landing," he wrote. "The feeling of power, smooth unworried power, is incredible." Later he was allowed to fly solo aerobatics at 25,000 feet, which he found "breathtaking". His next adventure was to fly in the rear seat of a Phantom Jet belonging to 43 Squadron. They flew twice over Balmoral at 400 feet, which he noted was an "unforgettable experience".

After five months, the Prince was awarded his wings and left the RAF. On his last evening, he was called upon to make a speech at a guest evening in the officers' mess. When he finished his fellow officers rose as one in a genuine, heartfelt standing ovation. In September, he headed to the Royal Naval College at Dartmouth to start his Royal Navy training proper.

A NAVAL ADVENTURE

Charles found learning seamanship and naval technology intense, especially as he had once again been put on a fast-stream six-week course – half the usual allocated time. After passing his exams at Dartmouth, he joined to the destroyer HMS *Norfolk* in Gibraltar. On his second day aboard, Charles recorded that he was greatly looking forward to "my first day at sea in one of Her Majesty's finest warships".

On the *Norfolk*, he was expected to gain a Bridge Watchkeeping Certificate in nine months, when a year would be more usual and he felt the pressure. "I believe in being well occupied and busy but I expect more is learned and accumulated by midshipmen who have longer to explore and investigate," wrote the Prince. "However, I did obtain my wings

Opposite: *The Prince of Wales pictured at Buckingham Palace, December 1971*

Prince Charles prepares for a flying lesson in a Jet Provost at RAF Cranwell

reasonably fairly ... and I passed the exams at Dartmouth, but I lacked that touch of professionalism which only comes after longer periods."

Despite his obvious talent and leadership qualities, he suffered periods of self-doubt. In one private letter to Lord Mountbatten he wrote: "I've been made to work extremely hard since I set foot in this mighty vessel. I stumble around the ship, falling down hatches and striking my head against bulkheads in an effort to find my way about ... I have been 'thrown in at the deep end' in the most obvious manner ... I'm afraid that I tend to suffer from bouts of hopeless depression because I feel that I'm never going to cope." But he did not let his insecurities show and proved popular with his peers.

In the autumn of 1971, Charles was based ashore at Portsmouth for several weeks. He stayed, at the invitation of his great uncle Lord Louis Mountbatten, at Broadlands, the stately home of the Mountbattens in nearby Hampshire. By this time Mountbatten, now in his seventies, was quite prepared to spend as much time as was required helping his great-nephew develop into a man fit for kingship. At this time Charles took to referring to Mountbatten as "honorary grandfather" and Mountbatten responded by calling Charles "honorary grandson".

A SUITABLE MATCH

Mountbatten also became the young Prince's confidant in matters of the heart and Charles began to discuss with him women he was drawn to. Among the young women in his circle was Lucia Santa Cruz, a friend from Cambridge who contacted Charles and said she had found "just the girl" for him and went on to make the arrangements for Charles

to meet Miss Camilla Shand. Camilla was attractive and, crucially, shared Charles's sense of humour. Like him she loved *The Goon Show* and Spike Milligan. She was individual, not too intense or serious, and smart.

Camilla came from the English landed gentry, on the edge of the royal circle, and was part of an aristocratic milieu that Charles understood. Her father, Bruce Shand, was a wine merchant and her mother, Rosalind, a member of the extremely rich Cubitt family, descended from Baron Ashcombe. There was also another unofficial family tie between her and the Windsors – her great-grandmother Alice Keppel had once been a mistress of his great-great-grandfather Edward VII. This amused the Prince.

It wasn't long before he was smitten and fell in love with Camilla. Charles felt at ease with her and felt sure that she could be the friend that he would want to love and spend his life with. Even better, she seemed to have the same feelings for him. By the late autumn of 1972 they had become inseparable.

Camilla, while being single and clearly fond of the heir to the throne, had previously been going out with a much sought-after cavalry officer, some nine years older than her, named Andrew Parker Bowles, whom she had dated since she was 18 in the hope that he would marry her.

In the autumn of 1972 Parker Bowles was posted to Germany and it appeared to Camilla that the relationship was finally over for good. She therefore felt free to enjoy a new relationship with the Prince. In the new year of 1973, Charles's next posting in the Royal Navy was due to separate them for eight months. In early December, he had joined his new ship, the frigate HMS *Minerva*, and was to sail on her to the Caribbean in January.

"After five months, the Prince left the RAF. On his last evening, he was called upon to make a speech in the officers' mess ... when he finished his fellow officers rose as one in a genuine, heartfelt standing ovation"

Opposite top: *Charles in an infantry colonel's uniform prepares to fire a bazooka during his visit to the Montgomery Barracks in West Berlin, Germany, October 1972*

Opposite bottom: *The Prince checks a weather report on the bridge of HMS Minerva, February 1973*

Prior to sailing, he invited Camilla to make a tour of inspection and then have lunch on board. She returned again the following weekend – "The last time I shall see her for eight months," he observed, sadly, in a letter to Mountbatten. But it was to be much worse than that. Andrew Parker Bowles, possibly motivated by Camilla's sudden independence and attraction to the Prince of Wales, returned to claim her and they became engaged in March 1973 – just two months after Charles had set sail. When the Prince came to hear of her renewed relationship with Parker Bowles he was deeply upset. Tom and Camilla wed in July 1973 in a large service that was attended by Princess Anne, Princess Margaret and the Queen Mother.

When the Parker Bowleses' first child Tom was born in 1974, Camilla asked Prince Charles to be a godfather. He happily accepted. Their friendship only became intimate once more after the birth of Camilla's daughter Laura in 1978. Depressed and lonely, she felt drawn to the Prince, who wasn't even engaged. Her husband, given his track record, was hardly in a position to complain. The affair was willingly agreed to by the Prince, and both believed it could lead nowhere: she was married, and one day so would he be – but never to a divorcee. So, Camilla became Charles's mistress.

Once in the Caribbean, Charles combined the roles of lowly junior naval officer and heir to the world's most famous throne. As a result, he was to attend scores of cocktail parties and, despite the "alcoholic haze", the Prince handled these very tricky diplomatic mazes with aplomb.

Charles's duties with the Royal Navy were becoming ever more varied and challenging and, by autumn 1974, he joined the Fleet Air Arm. After a helicopter conversion course in Yeovilton, Somerset, he was assigned to 845 Naval Air Squadron as a pilot on board the commando carrier HMS *Hermes*. There he was to spend the happiest four months of his naval career. He loved flying and, thanks mainly to Mountbatten, he had great affection for and loyalty to the Royal Navy.

He was duly assigned two helicopters that had bright-red nose- and tail-markings to denote that they were for his exclusive use, and they were subsequently maintained to the unique standards of the Queen's Flight. Once the Marines discovered this, Prince Charles became their favourite pilot, which was hardly a great endorsement of their confidence in the rest of the fleet's maintenance. Charles was a naturally gifted pilot. Towards the end of his time on HMS *Hermes* he wrote: "I had more fun flying than I ever had before. The flying was extremely concentrated, but there was masses of variety and interest; troop drills, rocket firing, cross-country manoeuvres (day and night), low-level transits, simulated fighter-evasion sorties, parachute-dropping flights and commando exercises with the Marines. There were no interruptions from any other source and as a result I ended up 'Hog of the Month' with about 53 hours in May!"

THE PRINCELY COMMANDER

Charles thought his next posting in the Royal Navy would be catastrophic; Mountbatten assured him it wouldn't be. On

"Charles loved flying and, thanks mainly to Mountbatten, he had great affection for and loyalty to the Royal Navy"

9 February 1976, he took command of his first ship – the coastal minehunter HMS *Bonnington* at Rosyth in Scotland. "The great and terrifying day had arrived at last," he recorded. "The whole prospect weighed heavily upon me as I drove across the Forth Bridge. There seemed so many things to worry about, particularly as I am not the sort of person who is endowed with supreme self-confidence."

For the next nine months the Prince sailed his command on the tedious duties that concerned a minesweeper's modest role in the Royal Navy. He remained most mindful that any slip-up would be seized upon by the press and cause not only personal humiliation but shame upon the Royal Family.

As a result of any such events remaining under wraps, and with no other disasters to report, the press ploughed on with the "action man" image and, after he had spent five years in the Royal Navy, the public's perception of the Prince had been completely transformed from that of a painfully shy young man to that of a naval hero. Headlines in the press spoke to the nation of: "FEARLESS, FULL OF FUN CHARLIE", "THE GET-UP-AND-GO PRINCE CHARLES" and "CHARLES, SCOURGE OF THE SEAS". This pleased the Palace, the Royal Navy, Mountbatten and, therefore, the Prince. It may also have pleased Prince Phillip, but if it did, it does not appear to have been recorded.

In December 1976, the Royal Navy's final report on Charles was written by Commander Elliott. "In spite of enormous outside pressure," it states, "Prince Charles has attained an excellent level of professional competence as a Commanding Officer. He has a natural flair and ability for ship handling and consequently his manoeuvres have been a pleasure to witness. Charles showed a deep understanding for his sailors, their families and their problems and as a result the morale of his ship has been of an extremely high order."

Perhaps he wasn't the sharpest of officers in his generation. There were certainly better navigators and finer sailors, and Charles's two most senior and experience lieutenants – Clare and Rapp – were naturally more suited to the sea; but, as a captain, Charles Windsor was a natural and the annals of British history have recorded him as such.

On the day that he left the Royal Navy, the officers and crew of his ship threw a lavatory seat around his neck and pushed him ashore in a wheelchair. As they proceeded down the quay at Rosyth, crews from every ship joined in the cheering as the Prince waved farewell to a gang, a club, an institution that had embraced him, protected him and loved him. And he had earned it all and deserved every bit of deep respect and affection that was shown to him. He had come a very long way from the bullied and bleak existence of Gordonstoun.

Opposite: *Charles with a colleague during his time with 845 Naval Air Squadron, January 1975*

CHAPTER FIVE

In Charles we trust
The philanthropic prince

At minimal cost to the public purse, the Prince of Wales has served as a great philanthropist and a champion of many causes, from the Prince's Trust and the Prince's Foundation to numerous foresighted environmental initiatives

The reign of King Charles III will inevitably appear short in length compared to that of his mother, Elizabeth II, and therefore may not go down in history as a remarkable one. But Charles's contribution through his lifetime of public service, especially as the Prince of Wales, has truly been outstanding. He will be remembered as a visionary man, a pioneer and somebody with the courage of his convictions – even if he has had to face ridicule for flying in the face of convention.

Apart from the necessary security bill and travel expenses when on official state business at home and abroad it should be noted that the taxpayer doesn't fund any of his lifestyle. He is effectively funded by the annual surplus from his landed estate, the Duchy of Cornwall, of which he is the steward.

The estate, which stretches over 135,000 acres and across 23 counties, mainly in the southwest of England, was last year estimated at £1 billion and Charles's net worth is said to be £306 million, according to a report by *Time* magazine. He is just a steward for this estate. The trust will pass to the Duke of Cambridge when he becomes Duke of Cornwall and beneficiary of the Duchy on Charles's ascension to the throne.

With the multimillions his Duchy of Cornwall estate generates for his personal use every year (last year it was £21.7 million, up 5 per cent on the previous year, and the tax paid voluntarily increased to £4.85 million), he might well live a cosseted existence. Why shouldn't he? The money is, after all, his, just as the money generated by, say, the Duke of Westminster's extensive property portfolio is his, or just as money generated by any other landed estate belongs to its owner. Unless there were to be some kind of communist-style land grab, that is the way it is.

Charles, therefore, could have happily lived the life of a playboy prince, a waster selfishly squandering his wealth on a debauched and lavish lifestyle. But he does not and, even though it is his "private income", the Prince has long chosen to be as open and transparent as possible.

From March 2017 through to March 2018, Charles and Camilla together undertook 620 official engagements in 45 counties across the UK and 15 foreign and Commonwealth countries around the world. The Prince visited ten Commonwealth countries in this year alone, supported by the Duchess on six of these visits. In his travels, sustainability and climate change – constant themes of his work for four decades – have been at the core of his message as he bids to raise awareness of the ways in which changes to our natural environment are having a negative impact on the world around us, particularly the case on low-lying islands, including across the Caribbean.

ENVIRONMENTAL CONCERNS

He attended, too, the Our Ocean Conference in Malta in October 2018, where his keynote address warned once again of the damage that is being caused by the dual threats of climate change and plastics pollution as humanity stretches nature to the limit. He had worked tirelessly to draw out the issue of religious tolerance and greater cultural cohesion, too, which he had addressed through his Easter message broadcast globally on Good Friday 2018, reaching a global audience of more than 10 million. In it he gave an emotional message of support for persecuted religious minorities, describing his compassion for "Christians who are suffering for their faith in many places around the world". He started the speech by

Below: *The Prince of Wales visits a local market on one of his annual trips to Devon and Cornwall, July 2017*

Below: *Charles visits the Caribbean following the hurricanes of September 2017*

saying, "I want to assure them that they are not forgotten and that they are in our prayers."

The Prince's detractors insist he is a drain on the public purse. The reality is in the relationship between private and public money, the taxpayer meets less than 10 per cent of the total costs for Charles and Camilla (excluding security costs) and those costs are usually for travel expenses when they are sent on official business and in a mode of transport selected by the government, not by the Prince.

The scope and diversity of the Prince's work is wide-ranging – from state occasions through to work to support the military, not to mention communities of every faith and of every ethnic origin, helping to bind all people together as a single United Kingdom. According to an independent study in 2017, the Prince contributed £1.4 billion of value to society in the last decade alone. His charities raised £170 million in a year, a figure they have repeatedly hit. On the environment, he practises what he preaches, too, with his household recording that 85 per cent of its energy now comes from renewable sources, including all of its electricity.

Despite all this almost obsessive devotion to duty, some still argue Charles is a pampered prince who has his elevated wealth and status only through the good fortune of his birth. If one chooses to ignore the facts about the man, it is easy enough to argue that point. After all Charles has a personal staff of over 120. There are valets who prepare his clothes and polish his shoes, chefs to indulge his every organic culinary whim, and a small army of estate workers. Gardening is one of his greatest passions, one that was sparked in childhood, playing with

Princess Anne outdoors and spending a lot of time with his grandmother, the Queen Mother, at the Royal Lodge in Windsor.

CHARLES THE PHILANTHROPIST

Charles has devoted his entire life to public duty, supporting the Queen in her role as head of state, as well as being a global philanthropist. With his Prince's Trust, which he started in 1976, having completed his duty in the Royal Navy, he had a bold idea that he believed would improve the lives of disadvantaged young people across the UK. The Prince's Trust delivers on that commitment and has been widely praised, having created more than 125,000 entrepreneurs since it started.

In March 2018 four of Prince Charles's charities were consolidated to create a new charity – the Prince's Foundation. The new charity will have its headquarters in Dumfries House in East Ayrshire. It incorporates the Great Steward of Scotland's Dumfries House Trust, the Prince's Foundation for Building Community, the Prince's Regeneration Trust and the Prince's School of Traditional Arts. The Prince's Foundation now focuses on improving the built environment, saving heritage, promoting culture and running community education projects UK-wide.

The Prince of Wales said of the move: "As I approach something of a milestone in my own life, I have had a chance to reflect on how best to ensure my charities continue to help those people and causes they were initially set up to serve, both now and for many years to come."

Charles believes in preserving what is good about the past and uses his clout and money to help rejuvenate areas of the country that would otherwise deteriorate. A case in point is

"Charles has devoted his entire life to public duty, supporting the Queen in her role as head of state, as well as being a global philanthropist"

Opposite: *Camilla and Charles walk through a guard of honour by representatives from the Fowey Gig Club, Cornwall, July 2018*

Above: *The Prince meets young chefs at Dumfries House in Ayrshire, May 2011*

the brilliant and visionary work he and his team have carried out in Scotland, where he is known as the Duke of Rothesay. In Ayrshire he was the driving for behind the rescue of Dumfries House a decade ago. In 2007, the stately home, nestled in the Ayrshire countryside, was about to be sold off – and with it much of the old furniture and antiques inside. So the Prince decided to use his various charities to buy it and save the house for the nation.

What he did at Dumfries House also helped save a community depressed by years of neglect after the closure of the coal mines which had caused may job losses, depressed the local economy, and seemed to start a slow demise of the entire community. Prince Charles opened the grounds of the stately home to the people free of charge. He employed local people to carry out the work to renovate the house and transform the grounds. He also built holiday cottages for rent and hired out the estate for weddings. He went further and built kitchens to train local people, established training courses for the unemployed in front-of-house hospitality, and now has school children in on the estate for special lessons on how food grows. He also built a sports hall for locals to hire, creating accommodation for scouts and guides and companies wanting space for team building.

His intervention has had a positive impact on the nearby villages of Cumnock and New Cumnock, as the profits from Dumfries House have paid for the renovation of the local town hall, and to rebuild the town's heated open-air swimming pool, which has also stimulated the construction of new affordable housing.

A PIONEERING LEGACY

When the time comes to assess his legacy, it is for his work as a pioneer and game-changer for which he will be best remembered. Even when he becomes king, I am confident he will do his best to find a way not to be suffocated by the limitations of the role and continue to strive to give a voice and platform to what he believes in.

He more than anyone still living is behind a global sustainability revolution to make world leaders – indeed us all – think more deeply about how we are treating nature and our planet, and to realise for the sake of future generations our lifestyles must change. He more than anyone has led the charge in changing how people think, and to realise, as he would say, "Right action cannot happen without right thinking."

In his 70 years the Prince has striven to make a real difference and to enlighten others. He has championed organic farming and spoken up for sustainable urbanism, emphasising the need for local character to be preserved. He has encouraged a more balanced approach to business and healthcare and a more benign holistic approach to science and technology. In doing so he has placed himself in the firing line and faced widespread criticism for daring to challenge the current orthodoxy and the conventional way of thinking.

It is clear that in Charles we are blessed to have a future king of high intelligence and drive. He is somebody who cares very deeply about the world and environment we live in, today and for the future. Charles, Prince of Wales, is fundamentally a decent man of integrity and honour who has always tried to put duty before himself.

CHAPTER SIX

Husband and father
The Diana years

Charles's fairy-tale wedding with his beautiful young bride ended in sadness – with neither the Prince nor the much-loved princess coming out of their divorce well – and ultimately tragedy

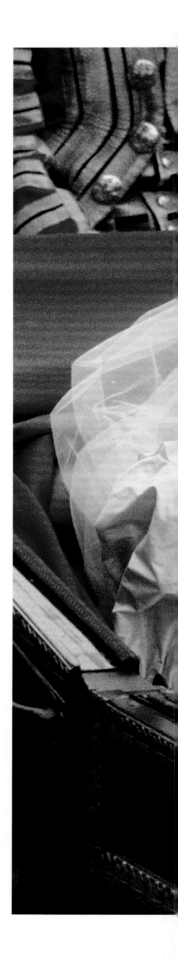

It was described as "the wedding of the century" and the fairy-tale romance. But sadly it was to end in acrimony and, ultimately, in tragedy.

The Prince of Wales married Lady Diana Spencer in St Paul's Cathedral on 29th July 1981, with Diana becoming Her Royal Highness The Princess of Wales. Nearly everyone in Britain will be able to remember where they were when the glass coach, pulled by two bay horses, arrived at the steps of St Paul's Cathedral and Lady Diana Spencer, looking every inch the radiant princess, stepped out in her billowing bridal train. The pomp and pageantry and sheer spectacle of the occasion are unmatched to this day.

Expectation had been building since the Prince and "Lady Di" announced their engagement five months previously. More than £100 million in souvenirs had flooded on to the market. A million people lined the wedding route from St Paul's to Buckingham Palace. Many had camped overnight and been treated on the eve of the wedding to an extravagant pyrotechnic display in Hyde Park, set to Handel's *Music for the Royal Fireworks*. The Prince had lit the first of 101 beacons and bonfires that blazed across the night's sky.

When, through loudspeakers, the crowd heard the Archbishop, Dr Robert Runcie, sum up their hopes with the words "This is the stuff of which fairy tales are made – the prince and princess on their wedding day", there were huge cheers that continued until long after the newly married couple glided past in the 1902 State Landau towards Buckingham Palace. In all, the ceremony cost an estimated £600,000 – the most expensive in British history.

TAKEN TO HEART

Diana Spencer came from an aristocratic lineage with long links with the Royal Family. She was born on 1 July 1961, at Park House on the Queen's estate at Sandringham, Norfolk, and lived there until the death in 1975 of her grandfather, the 7th Earl Spencer. It was then that the family moved to the Spencer family seat at Althorp House in Northamptonshire.

When the young Lady Diana was romantically linked with the Prince, she immediately became the darling of the media. To the world the marriage seemed to be a happy one. They had two sons: Prince William, born on 21 June 1982; and Prince Harry, born on 15 September 1984.

The Prince of Wales did not have the opportunity to spend as much time with the boys as he would have wanted. Often consumed by work, his time with them was limited, but he tried his best, sometimes spending time with his sons at Highgrove or Balmoral, the Queen's family's estate in Scotland. His sons revealed that Charles used to laugh "in all the wrong places" at their school plays and send them handwritten notes – apparently his penmanship was so appalling they couldn't tell if he was writing to praise them or to tell them off.

The couple became the most famous double act on the world stage. The Prince and Princess of Wales went on overseas tours and carried out many engagements together in the UK. Diana's photograph was rarely off the front pages. But the Princess's new-found fame brought with it tremendous stress and the eating disorder, bulimia, again began to take its toll on her.

The royal couple ride past crowds in central London following their wedding ceremony at St Paul's Cathedral, July 1981

"To the world the marriage seemed to be a happy one"

Opposite: Charles and Diana pose with their sons William and Harry in the wild flower meadow at Highgrove, July 1986

Nobody outside of the royal inner circle knew of the problems in the marriage. The Prince sought professional help for his wife but it was all in vain. After the birth of Prince Harry the marriage had irretrievably broken down and the couple began to live separate lives.

THE END OF THE FAIRY TALE

On 16 July, 1992, a book by Andrew Morton called *Diana, Her True Story* was published. Shrewdly, Diana had never met with its author face to face, which gave her plausible deniability. But it was clear to Charles and the Queen that Diana had colluded with the author, and the book proved damaging to both Charles and the Royal Family.

In the book, Diana depicted herself as a lamb to the slaughter on her wedding day – a 19-year-old virgin victimised by a bloodless cabal of royals. She exposed Charles's affair with his long-term love Camilla Parker Bowles, conveniently ignoring her own affairs with a string of suitors, including army officer Captain James Hewitt, who she later admitted she "loved and adored". In fact Diana refused to take any blame in the collapse of her marriage to the Prince or to acknowledge that her increasing hysteria, her constant self-harm, her suicide attempts and her rage-filled tantrums had any impact on the doomed relationship.

It took Prince Charles two years to give his version, sitting for a primetime interview with heavyweight journalist Jonathan Dimbleby, whose accompanying biography had the full co-operation of the Prince. This was an unprecedented move for a future king of England, and Charles, looking and sounding uncomfortable, admitted to cheating on Diana only after the marriage had "irretrievably broken down, us both having tried". But Charles couldn't win. The British public felt no sympathy for him; instead, they felt he'd debased himself and the monarchy.

Diana did it again in 1995, granting a wide-ranging interview to the BBC journalist Martin Bashir. Dressed in a smart black suit, eyes rimmed with kohl, Diana sought to blunt her own infidelity by volleying right back at Charles and Camilla. "There were three of us in this marriage," she said, damp eyes looking up from a bowed head. "So it was a bit crowded."

More than 25 million people watched the interview, which was announced on Charles's 47th birthday and aired on the Queen and Prince Philip's 48th wedding anniversary. In it, Diana also claimed to be a victim of Palace backstabbing, of orchestrated attempts to depict her as mentally ill, and as a target of sinister plots to get her to "go quietly". The knife twist: Diana claimed her husband wasn't fit for the British throne, his sole purpose in a life otherwise spent in purgatory. As for herself, Diana said she had no more humble aspiration than to be "a queen of people's hearts".

After the couple divorced at the Queen's insistence in 1996, Diana reinvented herself again, this time as a globetrotting humanitarian. Now her focus was on sick children and landmines and meeting with Mother Teresa rather than movie stars – but still, she fought hard to retain her title.

In the summer of 1997, Diana allowed paparazzi to catch her on vacation with Egyptian playboy Dodi al-Fayed, though

"The Prince sought professional help for his wife but it was all in vain ... the marriage had irretrievably broken down and the couple began to live separate lives"

*Prince Charles, Prince Harry,
Earl Spencer, Prince William and
the Duke of Edinburgh follow
Diana's coffin into Westminster
Abbey, September 1997*

she was fresh off a secret, two-year relationship with Hasnat Khan, a Pakistani heart surgeon she called "the love of her life". She'd even visited Khan's extended family in Pakistan in May 1996 – proof that she could live a private life when she chose.

In the weeks and months after Diana's death, chased through a Paris tunnel by paparazzi, the media came under much scrutiny, with many people blaming tabloid journalists and photographers for hounding the Princess to death. Even today – even as those who knew Diana admit that she used the press to cover her romance with al-Fayed, hoping to make Khan jealous – the prevailing narrative paints Diana as pure victim, hounded by a soulless media, consumed by our own prurient interest. Why couldn't we all just leave her alone?

On 9 December 1992, the Prime Minister, John Major, announced to the House of Commons that the Prince and Princess of Wales had agreed to separate. The marriage was dissolved on 28 August, 1996, although the Princess, as mother to the heir to the throne, was still regarded as a member of the Royal Family. She continued to live at Kensington Palace and to carry out her public work for a number of charities.

DEATH OF A PRINCESS

When the Princess was killed in a car crash in Paris on Saturday 31 August 1997, it fell on Charles to break the news to his young boys. "One of the hardest things for a parent to have to do is to tell your children that your other parent has died," Prince Harry said in BBC documentary. "How you deal with that, I don't know."

The Prince of Wales flew to Paris with her two sisters to bring her body back to London. The Princess lay in the Chapel Royal at St James's Palace until the night before the funeral.

On the day of the funeral, The Prince of Wales accompanied his two sons, aged 15 and 12 at the time, as they walked behind the coffin from The Mall to Westminster Abbey. With them were the Duke of Edinburgh and the Princess's brother, Earl Spencer.

The Prince of Wales asked the media to respect his sons' privacy, to allow them to lead a normal school life. In the following years Princes William and Harry joined their father on a limited number of official engagements in the UK and abroad.

Although Prince Harry later questioned the decision that led him to participate in the funeral procession as a 12-year-old, he seems to not fault his dad for what was undoubtedly a traumatic part of his childhood. "[Our dad] was there for us," said Harry. "He was the one out of two left, and he tried to do his best and to make sure that we were protected and looked after."

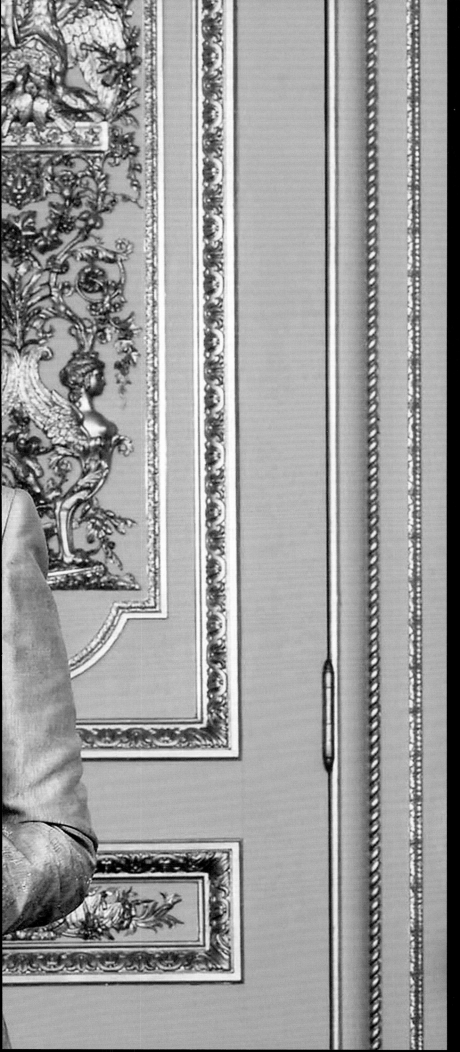

CHAPTER SEVEN

A fresh start
Charles and his new wife

More than three decades after they first met, Charles and Camilla finally married, part of a long process that has seen the Prince's wife establish her place in the Royal Family in recent years

More than two emotionally turbulent decades after the Prince had stood before the altar at St Paul's Cathedral and married Lady Diana Spencer, he made his vows to Camilla Parker Bowles. This time the ceremony was a civil one, in a room in Windsor Guildhall.

Any church involvement in the legal ceremony was not necessary, but given the monarchy's links with the established church – especially with Charles as the prospective Supreme Governor of the Church of England – the civil service was followed by a religious one of prayer and dedication. This took place at St George's Chapel, within the grounds of Windsor Castle, and was officiated by the sitting Archbishop of Canterbury, Dr Rowan Williams. After the wedding, Mrs Parker Bowles became known as Her Royal Highness The Duchess of Cornwall.

The couple were joined by around 800 guests and the service was followed by a reception at Windsor Castle hosted by The Queen. The Queen is passionate about horse racing and the date coincided with the Grand National in which she had a horse running, and she began her speech by saying she had two important announcements to make. The first was that Hedgehunter had won the race at Aintree; the second was that, at Windsor, she was delighted to be welcoming her son and his bride to the "winners' enclosure.

"They have overcome Becher's Brook and The Chair and all kinds of other terrible obstacles," said the Queen. "They have come through and I'm very proud and wish them well. My son is home and dry with the woman he loves." There was hardly a dry eye in the house.

WHEN CHARLES MET CAMILLA

The couple were introduced by his old university friend, Lucia Santa Cruz, who lived above the then Camilla Shand's apartment in London. He had been visiting Lucia in 1971 and she invited Camilla up for a drink, believing she and the Prince would hit it off.

It was there that Lucia had heard reference to the fact that Camilla's great-grandmother, Alice Keppel, had once been a mistress of his great-great-grandfather, Edward VII, which amused them both. "Now, you two, watch your genes," she said with a smile, referring to their ancestors' adultery.

In Camilla, Charles saw a woman with the strengths needed to handle the job of being his royal partner. She was not fazed by him or his royal status. By late autumn of 1972 they had become inseparable. Unfortunately for Charles, Camilla wasn't as devoted to him as he was to her. While extremely fond of Charles, she had previously dated cavalry officer Andrew Parker Bowles, nine years her senior, since she was 18. She was, unfortunately for Charles, still captivated by Parker Bowles. When he was posted to Germany in 1972 she felt the relationship was over for good and was free to enjoy her liaison with Charles.

But in the new year of 1973, Charles's next navy posting was to prove fatal for the romance. In early December he had joined his new ship, the frigate HMS *Minerva*, and was to sail on her to the Caribbean in January. He would be gone for eight months. Camilla joined him on a tour of the ship before it sailed and they had lunch on board. She returned the following weekend. He bemoaned the fact that it would be "the last time I shall see her for eight months".

Below: *Prince Charles and Camilla Parker Bowles leave the Service of Prayer and Dedication blessing their marriage at Windsor Castle, April 2005*

"When I broke the world-exclusive story of the royal engagement, the courtiers were ill-prepared"

Opposite: *The Prince and family watch highland games at the Braemar Gathering, September 2006*

It would be much worse than that as Andrew Parker Bowles had returned and with Charles far away Camilla and Andrew rekindled their relationship and became engaged in March 1973. It left the sensitive Prince emotionally drained.

He wrote to a friend that it seemed so cruel that fate should be this way. "Such a blissful, peaceful and mutually happy relationship... I suppose the feelings of emptiness will pass eventually." Charles and Camilla remained friends, over the next seven years, and she became one of his most trusted confidantes.

When the Parker Bowleses' first child, Tom, was born in 1975, Camilla asked the prince to be a godfather and he happily accepted. The intimacy between Charles and Camilla returned after the birth of Camilla's daughter Laura, when her husband Andrew continued with his philandering ways.

Camilla was drawn to the Prince again and an adulterous affair ensued. She was not the first married woman to move in royal circles and have an affair, nor was she to be the last. Charles knew fully the dangers in conducting an affair with a married woman but was prepared to take the risk. He knew in time he must marry a woman who was suitable to be his consort.

He was later to comment, "I've fallen in love with all sorts of girls and I fully intend to go on doing so, but I've made sure that I haven't married the first person I've fallen in love with. I think one's got to be aware of the fact that falling madly in love with someone is not necessarily the starting point to getting married. Marriage is basically a strong friendship, so I'd want to marry someone whose interests I could share."

THE CAMILLA QUESTION

The watershed moment came for Charles on the so-called "Camilla question", when he decided and announced that his relationship with her was "non-negotiable". He laid down a marker in the late 1990s that sent a message not only to the general public but to the mandarins at the palace and to the Queen herself. He still felt aggrieved at the way his "darling Camilla" was being treated but he made it abundantly clear he was not going to go along with it.

"All my life people have been telling me what to do," he said when asked about his relationship with Camilla Parker Bowles in a 1998 interview with trusted journalist Gavin Hewitt. "I'm tired of it. My private life has become an industry. People are making money out of it. I just want some peace."

When I broke the world-exclusive story of the royal engagement of the Prince of Wales and Camilla in the London *Evening Standard* – and, according to the prince's biographer and friend Jonathan Dimbleby, "bounced" Clarence House into issuing a formal announcement – the courtiers were ill-prepared. The wording of the statement that was released, long after the *Evening Standard* had broken the scoop, was simple enough. "It is with great pleasure that the marriage of HRH The Prince of Wales and Camilla Parker Bowles is announced," read the statement. "It will take place on Friday 8 April."

My inside source had been right on the money and we were both elated and relieved. In the weeks that followed, the extent to which my scoop had caught Charles's team off guard was woefully apparent. My story marked the start of a torrid time

"The marriage was the beginning of the end of 'the Camilla question' that had dogged the heir to the throne throughout his adult life"

Left: *Charles and Camilla visit the Singapore Botanic Gardens, October 2017*

for Clarence House officials, whose grasp on the finer and legal points of this royal wedding was exposed as being tenuous at best – if not altogether incompetent.

It started well enough. The ring, £100,000 worth of platinum and diamonds, had been a gift from the Queen. It was a 1930s Art Deco design, a central square-cut diamond with three smaller ones on either side, which had belonged to the Queen Mother and was one of her favourites. When asked how she felt, Camilla said she was just coming down to earth.

CONGRATULATIONS, AND ANGER

The Prime Minister sent congratulations on behalf of the government. The Queen and the Duke of Edinburgh were "very happy" and had given the couple their "warmest wishes". The Archbishop of Canterbury was pleased, too, that they had taken "this important step".

But soon critical newspaper headlines followed. The legality of the marriage was called into question; the impossibility of a church wedding turned Camilla into the House of Windsor's first "town-hall bride"; and, for a while in the early spring of 2005, barely a day passed without the revelation of some apparent monumental oversight or error by Prince Charles's team.

While they struggled to control the situation they were also forced to address one key question they might rather have ignored: what did William and Harry think about their father marrying the woman who ostensibly helped break up their mother's marriage, a woman their mother loathed with a passion? William gave his blessing, saying that both he and Harry were "delighted" at their father's happiness. Privately, their mood was more of acceptance than undiluted joy at the prospect of having Camilla as a stepmother.

Charles, William and Harry faced down the press when it was put to their father in public at a prearranged photo-call just seven weeks out from the wedding, when the boys enjoyed a skiing holiday with him in his favoured resort of Klosters, Switzerland. "How did he feel about the wedding?" a TV reporter asked. Charles knew the question was coming, as it had all been cleared with his communications team.

"Your Royal Highnesses," began the seasoned broadcaster Nicholas Witchell, shouting from behind the barrier separating the royals from the media. "It's eight days now to the wedding."

"You've heard of it, have you?" Prince Charles interrupted, with a fake smile.

Caught a little off guard, Witchell valiantly continued. "Can I ask how you are feeling and how, in particular, Princes William and Harry are feeling at the prospect of the wedding?"

"Very happy," replied Prince William immediately. "It'll be a good day."

"And Prince Charles, how are you feeling?" continued Witchell after a second or two of silence.

"As far as the Palace was concerned – and Charles too – the marriage was a triumph"

"It's a very nice thought, isn't it?" said Prince Charles, eventually, without a smile, then added a little sarcastically, "I'm very glad you've heard of it, anyway."

With that, he turned his head slightly away and, in a very quiet aside aimed solely at his sons, added, "Bloody people. I can't bear that man. He's so awful. He really is."

Charles, who hadn't seen the microphones in the snow before he had spoken so loosely, had been unaware that his curmudgeonly remarks were being picked up. It was a gaffe more befitting of his father, Prince Philip, than the usually media-savvy and careful Prince Charles.

It proved another low point in Charles's relationship with the British media. During the collapse of his marriage to Diana he had grown to loathe the cynicism of the tabloids for the blatant commercialisation of his personal misery.

A WEDDING TO REMEMBER

As far as the Palace were concerned – and Charles too – the marriage was a triumph. Camilla's deeply respected father, Major Bruce Stand, aged 88 at this time and ailing, stalled going to the doctor until after the wedding. He knew something was very wrong but was desperate to see his daughter, so often maligned, remarried.

The marriage was the beginning of the end of "the Camilla question" that had dogged the heir to the throne throughout his adult life.

Clarence House has inspired speculation about the Duchess of Cornwall and her future role. Charles's office had always insisted that the Duchess would be styled "Princess Consort" when the time comes, indicating that she would eschew the title of "Queen Consort" normally expected for the wife of a king.

The decision, announced in 2005 before the wedding, has not officially changed since then, even as the public attitude to the marriage has softened. A redesign of the couple's official website has seen the explicit statement about this role quietly removed, leading to reports that she could be given the title of "Queen" when the Prince of Wales accedes to the throne.

Since then Camilla, through hard work and the fact that time heals, has cemented her place in the Royal Family in recent years. The monarch marked her official 90th birthday by tidying up plans for her death and elevating the Duchess to the Queen's most senior advisory body, the Privy Council. It was, as ever, all done very quietly. But it is unprecedented in modern times for a royal wife not in direct line to the throne to be a member of the Privy Council – the cornerstone of the constitutional monarchy, enacting Acts of Parliament and advising the sovereign on the use of powers that do not formally go through Parliament. It also showed the esteem in which the Queen holds Camilla, and reflects the Royal Household's efforts to prepare the public for succession.

The Duchess of Cornwall and Prince Charles look on from the royal box at Royal Ascot, June 2013

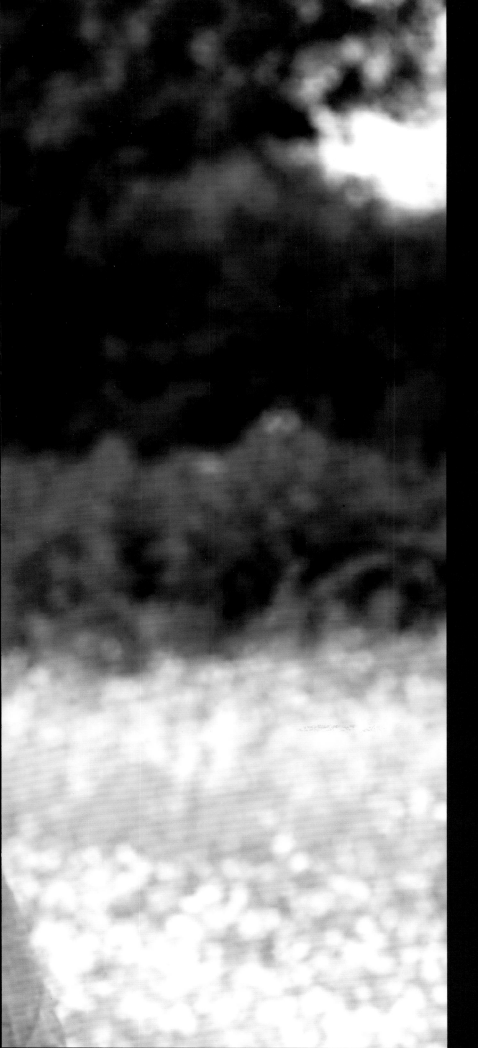

CHAPTER EIGHT

Philosopher prince
Saving the planet

A deep and thoughtful man, Prince Charles has developed a complicated philosophy that blends radical ecological policies with a much more conservative traditionalism

The Prince of Wales was in fine form as he walked up to the podium on 7 September 2016 on being named "Londoner of the Decade" at the *Evening Standard*'s Progress 1000 party, held at the Science Museum to honour the UK capital's innovators. He had thought long and hard about what he was going to say to a high-powered audience. What followed was one of the most significant, revealing and honest speeches of his career in public life.

"I have spent most of my life trying to propose and initiate things that very few people could see the point of, or thought were plain bonkers at the time," said the Prince. "Perhaps some of them are now beginning to recognise a spot of pioneering in all this apparent madness."

His remark drew laughter from the audience but, as ever, the Prince was deadly serious with his core message. "All forms of pioneering have moments that make you hold your breath and cross your fingers," he continued. "There is a good chance it could all go horribly wrong and there's a fine line between the success of a good, original idea and a complete disaster.

"If it fails, it fails, but at least you had a go – and I could always say one of my plants told me to do it! Starting my Duchy Originals food company 25 years ago was a case in point. When we launched the first organic oat biscuit there were tabloid headlines saying, 'A shop-soiled Royal'. People now tend to understand the point of, and enjoy, the organic food they once thought of as bonkers 25 years ago – and, through Duchy Originals, I have so far given away more than £14 million to charitable causes."

A NATIONAL TRUST

He went on to highlight how he established The Prince's Trust in 1976 amid social unrest and high levels of youth unemployment and how in 1983 he launched a business start-up plan.

"Again, people thought I'd gone mad – more mad! – to try and give grants to ex-offenders and other disadvantaged young people," he said. "But, since then, the Prince's Trust has supported over 825,000 of those vulnerable and disadvantaged young people to overcome their challenges, move into education or work or their own enterprises – thereby saving the public purse £1.4 billion in the process."

He also highlighted his Foundation for Building Community. "I believe it pays enormous social and environmental dividends if you go to the trouble of involving local people, with the right professional facilitators, in the design of the places where they live," he said. "The most successful communities mix the private with affordable housing; enclose green spaces within squares and communal gardens; provide good-quality housing integrated with walkable, mixed-use neighbourhoods, good public transport and an identity that fosters pride and a sense of belonging."

The Prince is not some tree-hugging fanatic. He is a pragmatist, a visionary and – as he proudly states – a pioneer. He is a deep-thinking man who works long hours to try to maximise his influence for the greater good of nature and humanity.

He has made many speeches and won many plaudits and awards for being a champion of the environment. His core philosophy is spelled out in his complicated 2010 book *Harmony: A New Way Of Looking At The World*, which he proudly describes as "a call to revolution". Throwing moderation to the wind, he comes out in favour of happiness, sustainable development and cities fit to live in, while opposing greed, ugliness and environmental catastrophe.

Throughout *Harmony* Charles describes the need to abandon a soulless modernity for a traditional spirituality. Essentially, it's a distillation of his beliefs – about nature, life,

Charles inspects produce during a reception to celebrate the 21st anniversary of Duchy Originals at Clarence House, September 2013

"The Prince is not some tree-hugging fanatic. He is a pragmatist, a visionary"

beauty and spirituality. It's also, as he says in his opening lines, "a call to revolution" and is therefore well worth a read.

Throughout the book, various dire and apocalyptic warnings follow about the state of the world, along with some predictable pops at modernism and factory-farming – significantly, he brackets the two together. Essentially, this philosopher prince thinks that we have become progressively divorced from nature and, in doing so, have lost something fundamental in ourselves. As a result, we now live in "an age of disconnection", cut off from the rhythms and the bounty of the world. The advantages this has brought us in material terms are, he reckons, dwarfed by the homogeneity, spiritual impoverishment and blinkered thinking that have come with it.

THE CONSERVATIVE REVOLUTIONARY

While this may be bold, it's also an intensely conservative philosophy – one that holds that mankind has gone increasingly awry since the Age of Reason, let alone mechanisation. The trouble, according to Charles, dates from when we started to see nature as something outside of ourselves; something unruly that needed to be tamed. The Prince's brand of neo-Puritanism could only have been incubated in a pretty rarefied environment. However, there is no doubt that Charles would deny that his instincts face backwards rather than forwards.

There is much to admire about the way the Prince has highlighted the horrors of factory farming and his belief that people, rather than town planners, are often the best judges of what sort of environment suits them. His work against single-use plastics was both ahead of its times and crucial for the future of our planet that many in the popular media have now woken up to.

In January 2018 the Prince of Wales attended a meeting to discuss plastic waste at the British Academy in London at which he said the nightmare of plastic in oceans will only get worse. He spoke of his "deep frustration" at the world ignoring the problem and called on companies to make changes to cut their plastic waste.

"The nightmare result of eight million tonnes of plastic entering the ocean every year is set to get worse rather than better," he said. "We cannot, indeed must not, allow this situation to continue... I do fervently pray that you will all do your utmost to work together in the coming year to make real, substantial progress. It could not be more critical that you succeed."

Each year more than 300 million tons of plastic are produced globally, and at least eight million tonnes ends up in the sea. It is estimated that there is now a 1:2 ratio of plastic to plankton and, left unchecked, plastic will outweigh fish by 2050. Not only is the floating haze of scum unsightly, it is also swallowed by marine animals that cannot digest it. Chemicals leach into the water, and it has been shown that even humans who eat seafood ingest more than 11,000 pieces of micro-plastic each year.

Charles, long known for his interest in environmental causes, said he had taken some encouragement from the fact that the legacy of plastic in the environment is now very much on the global agenda and in the public consciousness. This change by the public is in no small way due to his tireless work to educate and inform people as he goes about his daily business at home and abroad.

Charles has had a huge impact on the world stage, spreading his messages. He has risked the wrath of those who

"Throwing moderation to the wind, the Prince comes out in favour of happiness, sustainable development and cities fit to live in, while opposing greed, ugliness and environmental catastrophe"

Above: *Senior figures gather during the United Nations Climate Change Conference, November 2015*

Left: *The Prince looks around an "eco house" at the Ideal Home Show, March 2014*

say he should not be political or partisan by courageously speaking out on the issue of climate change. The Prince believes global warming is the greatest threat that humanity faces and in November 2015 he joined world leaders for the COP (Conference of Parties) 21 meeting in Paris – the 21st United Nations Climate Change Conference.

On the podium the Prince opened the conference along with the United Nations climate chief, Christiana Figueres, and the French Foreign Minister, Laurent Fabius. Charles did not hold back. "On an increasingly crowded planet, humanity faces many threats, but none is greater than climate change," he told delegates from 195 countries. "It magnifies every hazard and tension of our existence. It threatens our ability to feed ourselves, to remain healthy and safe from extreme weather, to manage the natural resources that support our economies, and to avert the humanitarian disaster of mass migration and increasing conflict."

Urging negotiators to end fossil-fuel subsidies and spend the money on sustainable energy instead, he said: "We must act now. Already we are being overtaken by other events and crises that can be seen as greater and more immediate threats. But, in reality, many are already, and will increasingly be, related to the growing effects of climate change."

The Prince, who also spoke at the landmark Copenhagen climate conference in 2009, then told officials that the climate-change crisis had become much more urgent in the intervening six years. "The whole of nature cries out at our mistreatment of her," he said. "If the planet were a patient, we would have treated her long ago. You, ladies and gentlemen, have the power to put her on life support, and you must surely start the emergency procedures without further procrastination."

SAVING THE PLANET

The Prince is adamant that governments must act now to save our planet from disaster. He says he knows they have the technology and money to tackle the problem, but so far have lacked the conviction and the framework to use them wisely and at scale.

What is exciting about Charles is that he is a trailblazer. He is not a figurehead who jumps on bandwagons when they become trendy. He has been delivering speeches for decades on his core subjects such as climate change and polluting our planet. Way back on 6 March 1989, he was addressing delegates at the Saving the Ozone Layer World Conference, where he spelt out the doomsday scenario we faced then when few wanted to listen.

"Since the Industrial Revolution, human beings have been upsetting that balance [of nature], persistently choosing short-term options and to hell with the long-term repercussions," he said. Indeed, he faced an avalanche of criticism in the 1970s for even daring to raise these heartfelt concerns. But raise them he did.

"Most critics imagined that I somehow wanted to turn the clock back to some mythical golden age when all was a perfect rural idyll. But nothing could be further from the truth," he wrote in his tome *Harmony*.

Nearly 30 years later, he is still using his influence to urge mankind to take effective action to save our sick planet before it is too late, and he should be applauded for it.

CHAPTER NINE

Commonwealth champion
The global ambassador

When Charles was formally announced as the successor to the Queen as Head of the Commonwealth, it was the deserved reward for more than 40 years of work in service of the institution

In February 2018, the BBC went public with a story that many people had long suspected to be the case – that the Commonwealth leaders had secretly begun to consider who might succeed Her Majesty the Queen as its next head. Prince Charles was not necessarily the number-one choice, the BBC reported, and its reporters had seen documents to prove it.

Worse still on BBC Radio 4's *Today* it was wrongly claimed that Charles was not all that keen on the job anyway and that the Commonwealth did not mean as much to him as it did to his mother. He was understandably peeved. The reality is the exact opposite.

For Charles has been a very active supporter of the Commonwealth for more than 40 years. Understandably, for this entire time, he has been in the shadow of his mother, who succeeded her father, King George VI, as its head when she ascended to the throne. But the Queen, due to her age, hasn't carried out long-haul flights for several years and it is Charles, supported by his sons and siblings, who do much of the heavy lifting when it comes to overseas Commonwealth visits.

A GLOBAL CITIZEN

He cares deeply about the organisation and what it stands for, after all it represents 2.3 billion people and 53 nations – a third of the world's population. "I have long had an instinctive sense of the value of the Commonwealth," he said in a 2000 visit to Trinidad. He has often spoken of the "pivotal role" that the Commonwealth has to play in safeguarding our planet.

Charles shows his support through official visits, military links, charitable activities and other special events. In April 2018 in Brisbane he opened the highly successful Commonwealth Games and then toured Australia before flying back for the Commonwealth summit in London and Windsor. Since 1969, the Prince has visited more than 44 Commonwealth countries, and in November 2018, just ahead of his 70th birthday, he will tour three more: the Gambia, Ghana and Nigeria.

When he addressed the Commonwealth Heads of Government Meeting (CHOGM) in London, he stressed that its leaders must listen to the views of the next generation. It was the kind of vision and leadership expected of a future head of the Commonwealth. Charles recognises that the institution can be a force for good and most recently he has led the charge for island states that face being wiped out by a rise in sea levels with his Blue Economy initiative. In growing the Blue Economy he hopes to combat poverty and accelerate prosperity in these under-threat regions.

The problem for the monarchy is that the position of head is not enshrined in the constitution. It is symbolic, with no formal powers. Her Majesty the Queen worked hard in private to ensure her eldest son and heir, the Prince of Wales will succeed her as head of the Commonwealth. It is a responsibility that she says she has cherished – but it is not one that Charles would have inherited automatically.

As the national broadcaster, the BBC was right to discuss the matter but it was also stirring the pot ahead of the CHOGM. It was true, prior to a formal decision on who would be the next head of the organisation, that the Prince was by no means assured of securing the position. He was always going to rely on Commonwealth leaders giving him their formal blessing and wanting him to replace his mother. That said, there was little

Opposite: *The Prince of Wales and Duchess of Cornwall visit the Sri Mahamariamman Temple in George Town, Malaysia, November 2017*

Above: *Charles and Camilla in Penang, Malaysia, November 2017*

Left: *The Prince poses with the likes of Australian Prime Minister Tony Abbott and President of Sri Lanka Mahinda Rajapaksa at the Commonwealth Heads of Government Meeting, November 2013*

"Charles will stamp his mark on the Commonwealth now that his position as its future head has been confirmed"

doubt, after years of distinguished service, that there were few better qualified for the albeit titular role.

THE QUEEN'S SINCERE WISH

On 20 April 2018 Charles took another step closer to the chalice when Commonwealth leaders backed the Queen's "sincere wish" to recognise that her heir, the Prince of Wales, would one day succeed her as the next Head of Commonwealth. Theresa May, the British Prime Minister, announced the decision from the 53 Commonwealth Heads of Government after private deliberations at Windsor Castle, where Commonwealth leaders said they had reached an agreement to honour Her Majesty's "vision, duty and steadfast service" to the institution.

Speaking at a press conference after the retreat, Prime Minister May said that the Commonwealth itself exists in "no small measure because of the vision, duty and steadfast service of Her Majesty in nurturing the growth of this remarkable family of nations".

The Prime Minister continued. "On behalf of all our citizens I want to express gratitude for everything Her Majesty has done and will continue to do," she said. "Today we have agreed that the next head of the Commonwealth will be His Royal Highness Prince Charles, the Prince of Wales. His Royal Highness has been a proud supporter of the Commonwealth for more than four decades and has spoken passionately about the organisation's unique diversity. It is fitting that he will one day continue the work of his mother, Her Majesty the Queen."

When it was finally and formally announced the Prince was typically self-effacing. "I am deeply touched and honoured by the decision of Commonwealth heads of state and government that I should succeed the Queen, in due course, as head of the Commonwealth," he declared. "Meanwhile, I will continue to support Her Majesty in every possible way, in the service of our unique family of nations."

A UNANIMOUS DECISION

Presidents and prime ministers from across the world convened to finalise plans for the future of the Commonwealth, enjoying the hospitality of the Queen's home at the end of a week that had seen senior members of the Royal Family out in force. President of Ghana, Nana Akufo-Addo, said the decision was reached by "strong consensus", while Theresa May insisted it was unanimous. Grenada's Prime Minister, Keith Mitchell, said he had been convinced the decision was a good one thanks to his belief that the young men of the Commonwealth need a strong male role model.

It was made clear, however, that the decision was a one-off, and the leaders spelled it out that the ruling did not apply to Charles's own heirs, Prince William and Prince George, who would not be automatically in line to hold the office. It would remain, they said, a non-hereditary position.

That said, the Queen had left nothing to chance. The day before the ruling, as she spoke at the official opening of the CHOGM at Buckingham Palace, she made a heartfelt address spelling out for the first time her hopes for the future of the Commonwealth, and offering her unadulterated support to her son in the role.

"It is my sincere wish that the Commonwealth will continue to offer stability and continuity for future generations, and will decide that one day the Prince of Wales should carry on the

"Charles believes that the modern Commonwealth has a vital role to play in building bridges between our countries, fairer societies and a more secure world around them"

important work started by my father in 1949," she told the leaders gathered. There is little doubt that the Queen's public words galvanised the world leaders into pushing through the decision.

"We are certain that, when he will be called upon to do so, he will provide solid and passionate leadership for our Commonwealth," Joseph Muscat, Prime Minister of Malta, said of the Prince in the same ceremony. Later that day, Malcolm Turnbull, the Australian Prime Minister, confirmed that his country "strongly supports the continuation of the king or queen of the United Kingdom as the head of the Commonwealth," he stated, unequivocally. "Prince Charles in time will succeed his mother."

Speaking to media, Justin Trudeau, the Canadian Prime Minister, said, "I very much agree with the wishes of Her Majesty that the Prince of Wales be the next head of the Commonwealth." And Ralph Regenvanu, the Foreign Minister of the Pacific state of Vanuatu, disclosed, "We see it almost naturally that it should be the British Royal Family because it is the Commonwealth after all."

Others had expressed frustration that the issue had overshadowed more important discussions. Tevita Tu'i Uata, Tonga's trade minister, told ITV News that people in his country "are drowning" due to rising sea levels. "Maybe sorting out who is going to lead the Commonwealth may be also an issue," he said, "but it's not as pressing an issue to [Tonga] as taking care of climate change."

THE PRINCE REGENT

Going forward, the Prince is expected to represent the Queen in the honorary role at future Commonwealth meetings, the next of which will take place in Rwanda in 2020, having previously attended the meeting four times: in Edinburgh in 1997, Uganda in 2007, Sri Lanka in 2013 and Malta in 2015 when he appeared *with* the Queen, rather than on his own.

Also, Charles's sons and their wives, the Duke and Duchess of Cambridge and the Duke and Duchess of Sussex, are expected to support the Prince and his wife the Duchess of Cornwall in championing the Commonwealth and the Royal Family's links to it.

Indeed, the Queen appointed her grandson Prince Harry Commonwealth Youth Ambassador in April, which lays the path for his future. His role, supported by his wife Meghan, is to convene young leaders from across the Commonwealth to discuss how the organisation can work best for them.

Charles will also stamp his mark on the Commonwealth now that his position as its future head has been confirmed. For the Prince, the bottom line is that the Commonwealth is a fundamental feature of his life. His first Commonwealth visit was to Malta when he was just five years old. He has, over time, spoken to many of the giants of the club: Sir Robert Menzies, Kwame Nkrumah, Sir Keith Holyoake, Jomo Kenyatta, Pierre Trudeau, Kenneth Kaunda, Julius Nyerere and Lee Kuan Yew.

But for Charles it is not applauding past successes; for he believes that the modern Commonwealth has a vital role to play in building bridges between our countries, fairer societies within them and a more secure world around them. He hopes his role will enable member states not only to revitalise the bonds with each other but also to give the Commonwealth a "renewed relevance to all citizens", finding practical solutions to their problems and giving life to their aspirations. That way, he believes, the Commonwealth will be a cornerstone for the lives of future generations.

After all the Prince of Wales has never been one for applauding past successes. He believes that the modern Common wealth has a vital role to play in building bridges between countries, fairer societies within them and a more secure world around them.

CHAPTER TEN

Shadow King
Monarch without a crown

With Her Majesty The Queen now well into her nineties, Prince Charles is taking over an increasing number of responsibilities that would usually be the province of the sovereign in what has become a unique royal job share

As we approach the end of 2018, a more accurate description of Charles's role is "Shadow King". It is he, not Her Majesty Queen Elizabeth II, who is now doing most of the "heavy lifting" for the monarchy at home and abroad while representing his 92-year-old mother.

The Queen – who will turn 93 in April 2019 and who once said she has to be "seen to be believed" – has not travelled on long-haul flights on state business since her visit to Australia in 2011. Her last state visit overseas was a short hop on a private jet to Germany in June 2015. The previous year she paid a state visit to France and went by Eurostar. The Queen now restricts her journeys to short flights, "away-days" by royal train, commercial railway or car, all within the United Kingdom.

Her once ever-present "liege man", her loyal consort and husband of more than 70 years, His Royal Highness the Duke of Edinburgh, turned 97 in June 2018 and has all but retired from public life having, as he put it, "done his bit". With perfect timing, he walked off the royal stage in a summer downpour on 2 August 2017 at Buckingham Palace, raising his bowler hat in acknowledgement to the Plymouth Band of the Royal Marines who played "For He's a Jolly Good Fellow".

As he went back inside he made one of his trademark quips, joking with two Royal Marine corporals, who had run 1,664 miles over 100 days as part of the 1664 Global Challenge (named after the year that the Royal Marines were founded), that they should be "locked up" for the corps' fundraising efforts.

A JOB-SHARE MONARCHY

This was undoubtedly a moment that marked the end of an era. His departure from public life, however, was a watershed moment for his son the Prince of Wales. For, with his father no longer ever present at the Queen's side, Charles would now be the lead man in the unfolding royal story.

When he eventually ascends the throne on the death of his mother, he will be the oldest person ever to become our monarch. None of this concerns him, or, for that matter, ever has. He has always said his getting the "top job" is "in the lap of the gods".

Some close to the monarch say that, if she reaches 95 she will mark it by officially allowing Charles to take over the stewardship of her reign by transferring her executive powers to him and making him Prince Regent until her death, when he will become king.

This would enable her to fudge the issue of not fulfilling her Coronation Oath to God and her people to serve as queen regnant until her death, something she told the then Archbishop of Canterbury, Dr George Carey, when he went to see her when he resigned in her Golden Jubilee year of 2002. "Resignation?" she pondered. "That's something I can't do."

Since then the monarch has marked her Diamond and Sapphire jubilees. She has already surpassed her great-great-grandmother, the Empress of India, Queen Victoria, and become the oldest and longest-reigning monarch. In truth, with the Queen now well into her tenth decade, senior officials within the Royal Household confirm that Prince Charles is, effectively, already a king in all but name.

He already takes on many of her responsibilities and, now that she does not travel overseas, his royal tours representing her across the globe are state visits. It is, in effect, a job-share monarchy, with the heir leading the way for the House of Windsor, not following.

Opposite: *The Queen and Prince Philip arrive for the state banquet in their honour in Berlin, Germany – Her Majesty's last state visit overseas, June 2015*

REGAL DREAMS

The Prince of Wales has always been consistent about his position. "Sometimes you daydream about the sort of things you might do," he told Jonathan Dimbleby in 1994, while talking about becoming king one day. "I think you could invest the position with something of your own personality and interest but obviously within the bounds of constitutional propriety."

The only time he went further was in 1998, when he was forced to react to claims that he would be "pleased" if the Queen abdicated. He was irritated at the impertinence of the suggestion in the tabloids. "I begin to tire of needing to issue denials of false stories about all manner of thoughts which I am alleged to be having," he said.

One of the most visually significant moments that showed a monarchy in transition happened last November on Remembrance Sunday. His head bowed, the Prince of Wales, not the Queen, led the nation in commemorating our war dead. As he laid the first wreath – the nation's wreath – of red poppies at the foot of the Cenotaph memorial in Whitehall, *he* took the lead role. As ever, he had performed his duties with aplomb but, unequivocally, this was a watershed moment in his developing royal journey.

A few minutes earlier he had led out seven members of the Royal Family, all bedecked in military uniform. His sons, William and Harry, his siblings Anne, Andrew and Edward, and his mother's first cousin and grandson of King George V, the Duke of Kent, dutifully followed him and then stood in silence. Charles, in front of them, waited patiently for his signal to perform. The unmistakable chimes of Parliament's Big Ben and a gun salute marked the beginning of the two-minute silence. Another gun salute, followed by the Reveille played immaculately by nine white-gloved buglers of the Royal Marines' Portsmouth Band, bedecked in Number 1 Full Dress of full-length, dark-blue greatcoats with the white Wolseley-pattern helmets, signalled that the impeccably observed silent tribute was at an end.

It was 12 November 2017 – the day after Armistice Day and just two days shy of Charles's 69th birthday and the start of his milestone 70th year. Less than a hundred metres away on a Whitehall balcony, the Queen, wearing a spray of poppies held in place by Queen Mary's gleaming Dorset bow brooch, keenly observed proceedings, watching her eldest son's every move with a sharp eye. Alongside her, in his uniform as Lord High Admiral, was World War II veteran Prince Philip, then aged 96, protected from the autumn chill by his heavy Royal Navy winter greatcoat. Next to the royal couple stood Prince Charles's second wife, all in black, the 70-year-old Duchess of Cornwall. It had been a definite move by the Queen to authorise her heir to carry out the job and it was certainly not a decision taken lightly.

THE TRANSFER OF RESPONSIBILITY

In the months leading up to this symbolic moment the Prince of Wales had slowly but surely been taking on a number

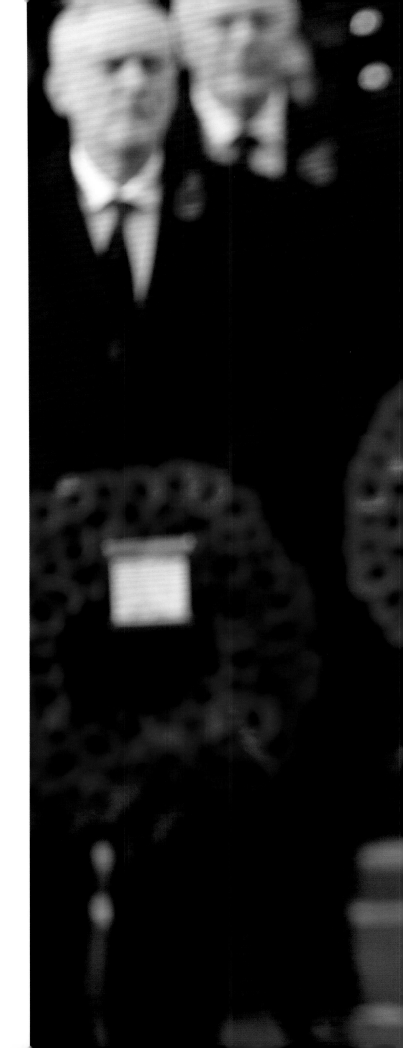

"His head bowed, the Prince of Wales led the nation in commemorating our war dead ... this was a watershed moment in his developing royal journey"

The Queen and Prince Charles reside over the State Opening of Parliament, June 2017.

"Charles will play a dual role, standing in and covering for the monarch where necessary"

of the Queen's more physically taxing engagements at her request. In 2017 the Prince clocked up 374 UK engagements and 172 abroad, making him the busiest member of the Royal Family with a grand total of 546 engagements. He did the most travelling, too.

For the Prince in the coming years it was going to get busier as more and more he did the heavy lifting for the ageing sovereign. As ever, he carried out his duties with the minimum of fuss. It was, as he saw it, his duty to do so as her "liege man", as he had sworn to be before 4,000 guests inside the medieval walls of Caernarfon Castle at his investiture as Prince of Wales in 1969. Back then he had received the insignia as the 21st Prince of Wales and, along with it, the right to use the heraldic badge of the title that bears the motto, "*Ich Dien*" – "I Serve" in German – on the ribbon below the coronet and his feathers.

This engagement at the Cenotaph was perhaps Charles's most "kingly" to date. It was, perhaps, also the most piquant as Charles was surrounded by the political, military and religious establishment and with millions watching the broadcast live on BBC television around the country. What

unfolded was an unmistakably historic image, the clearest visual sign to date that the British monarchy was undergoing a seamless transition from monarch to her eldest son.

Charles will, in this interim period before his ascension to the throne, play a dual role, standing in and covering for the monarch where necessary. His sovereign moment was over in a matter of minutes and he had, as ever, performed his duty with equanimity.

Announcing the decision to entrust the job to Prince Charles a few weeks earlier, Buckingham Palace had said that the reason was that the Queen wished to be by her husband's side on the balcony and had asked her heir to lay a wreath instead. Make no mistake, however, this moment marked the beginning of a gradual transfer of monarchical responsibility from the reigning queen to the heir apparent.

The Queen may still be in authority, but this moment marked a passing on of obligation, if not power. Inevitably, such designated responsibility – whether Buckingham Palace officials accept it or not – gave the perception of a transfer of power and an expectation of a new leader waiting in readiness in the wings.

CHAPTER ELEVEN

Ecological awareness
Caring for the environment

Assorted charities concentrate on specific ecological concerns that have been championed by the Prince of Wales for decades, be it global pollution or animal welfare

A natural selection

THE GREEN PIONEER

Prince Charles's forthright views on ecology and the environment have proved to be perceptive and prescient

The Prince's holistic concerns about the environment are summed up in his 2010 book *Harmony*. "I have tried for 25 years to encourage social and environmentally responsible business, to suggest a more balanced approach to certain aspects of medicine and healthcare; more rounded ways of educating our children; and a more benign, 'whole-istic' approach to science and technology," he writes. "The trouble is that in all these areas I have been challenging the accepted wisdom; the current orthodoxy and conventional way of thinking, much of it stemming from the 1960s but with its origins going back over 200 years."

In the book, he draws connection between various disciplines that have always fascinated him – religion, architecture, education, medicine – and points out ways in which they are all linked to a primal, natural order that chimes with the planet's ecology. "What I have been trying to demonstrate is that all of these subjects are completely inter-related," he writes, "and that we have to look at the whole picture to understand the problems we face."

Nature, he says, works on a series of interlocking cycles, or natural cadences that ensure that life is maintained. "Fashions may change, ideologies may come and go, but what remains certain is that Nature works as she has always done, according to principles that we are all familiar with. Nutrients in soils are recycled, rain is generated by forests, and life is sustained by the annual cycles of death and rebirth. Every dead animal becomes food for other organisms. Rotting and decaying twigs and leaves enrich soils and enable plants to grow, while animal waste is processed by microbes and fungi that transform it into yet more vital nutrients. And so Nature replaces and replenishes herself in a completely efficient manner, all without creating great piles of waste."

For Charles, intensive industrialisation over the course of the last two and a half centuries has disrupted the cycles of this natural process, with disastrous effects for the planet and its inhabitants. "It is clear that on every front mankind is overexploiting nature; the more we waste, the more we have to use our irreplaceable natural resources and prejudice the lives of our grandchildren," he wrote in a 2010 article for *Vogue* magazine. "This can be seen in the depletion of our ocean's fish stocks, not to mention the destruction of the world's rainforests. When you add the threat of global warming caused by greenhouse gas emissions, few can doubt that our lifestyles will need to change if we are to avoid environmental catastrophe."

It is why the Prince has worked hard to push society down a path that avoids such catastrophe. As a patron of assorted ecological charities, and a supporter of many more, he has raised dozens of environmental issues – from the benefits of organic farming to the perils of single-use plastic; from promoting natural fabrics to supporting the preservation of indigenous breeds of British livestock. He has been an active proponent of recycling and a people-centred town planning, encouraging architects and civil engineers to reuse existing buildings rather than demolishing and building anew.

"If people are encouraged to immerse themselves in Nature's grammar and geometry – discovering how it works, how it controls life on Earth, and how humanity has expressed it in so many great works of art and architecture – they are often led to acquire some remarkably deep philosophical insights into the meaning and purpose of Nature and into what it means to be aware and alive in this extraordinary universe. This is particularly so in young people and the results of such immersion are as heartening as they are surprising. They help to point to the changes in thinking that we need to make to achieve the wider vision of a Sustainability Revolution."

The Prince Of Wales and the Duchess Of Cornwall join BBC science and nature presenter Kate Humble at her farm in Monmouth in July 2015

Sky impact investment

SKY OCEAN VENTURES

Sky is fighting the ecological disaster of
single-use plastics with Sky Ocean Ventures

sky ocean ventures

Right: *Sky's Group CEO Jeremy Darroch is leading the organisation's campaign against plastic pollution*

I t was after Sky News began broadcasting bulletins about the excessive amounts of plastic being discovered on the world's beaches that the media corporation decided to launch Sky Ocean Rescue. This initiative was created in January 2017, initially as a way of raising awareness about the amount of plastic that is constantly being dumped in the sea – the equivalent of a lorry load every minute. A commitment to eradicating plastic pollution has since become central to the company's practices, aligning it with the tireless campaigning work of Prince Charles.

The Sky Ocean Rescue campaign reached 10 million people in the UK, but Sky's work in this area is far from finished. It has also created Sky Ocean Ventures, a £25 million innovation fund that will invest in promising new ideas to help people and businesses move on from plastic. Again, the influence of Prince Charles is integral.

"Sky Ocean Ventures is a bold new creation that will support breakthrough thinking and invest in promising new ideas that will help turn off the plastics tap," explains Jeremy Darroch, Sky Group's CEO. "It is time businesses stopped dumping harmful plastic into the sea and instead started pumping more money into innovation. We look forward to working with other like-minded organisations who can help us find and support innovators who are developing products, materials and business models that will create meaningful change. We are a big voice and we can use that voice to lobby and to shine a spotlight on some of the issues the ocean is facing. For us, it's part of doing the right thing."

Prince Charles has frequently raised the issue of plastic during sessions of the International Sustainability Unit, the organisation he founded in 2010. During sessions, His Royal Highness would deliver powerful warnings about the dangers of plastic in our seas. Darroch cites these as a "catalyst" for transforming Sky's thinking about sustainability issues. His

Royal Highness has advocated a process of working with business to form coalitions that build solutions, and Sky believes that – as an innovative company with a wide customer base – it is uniquely positioned to not just raise understanding of the issue but to also help develop impactful solutions through supporting mission-driven entrepreneurs.

As Darroch's involvement demonstrates, Sky's anti-plastics campaign comes from the very top of the company and the business has an exemplary reputation on championing environmental issues. Ten years ago, Sky became the world's first carbon-neutral media company and its Sky Rainforest Rescue initiative has raised more than £9 million and helped save one billion trees in Brazil. Since the focus moved to the ocean and the plastic crisis, Sky has pledged to eradicate all single-use plastics from its operations, products and supply chains by 2020. Sky has provided every employee with a refillable bottle, saving approximately 450,000 plastic bottles a year and has also developed the Sky Soundbox, which is the company's first product to have single-use plastic-free packaging – all further new Sky products will have packaging that is free of single-use plastic.

But it is the establishment of Sky Ocean Ventures that really moves the conversation along from the problem to the solutions. With this initiative, Sky has committed £25 million of capital and is leveraging its reach to build an innovation ecosystem designed to unearth and incubate early-stage ideas that will reduce plastics leakage. It has formed partnerships with academic institutions and has also created an advisory board that includes pre-eminent scientists, activists, and entrepreneurs such as Jonathan Baillie, the chief scientist of National Geographic Society, Emily Penn, the sailor and ocean activist, and Kristian Teleki, the Director of Sustainable Initiative at the World Resources Institute.

Left: *Sky is promoting an anti-plastics campaign in partnership with the Premier League.*

Right: *Prince Charles meets the Sky Ocean Campaign during the 2018 Commonwealth summit*

Sky is also working with the Premier League to use their global reach and appeal to raise awareness of the environmental issues caused by plastic. The Premier League and Sky will promote Sky Ocean Rescue to inspire Premier League clubs and fans across the world to take positive action and reduce their single-use plastic intake, making small changes that will have a big impact.

In May 2018, Sky Ocean Ventures announced a partnership with the National Geographic Society and National Geographic Partners that will help develop the best innovative ideas in plastic reduction through a series of global competitions. "This will combine our scale and voices and allow us to set up programs to find audacious innovations that help solve the design and business model challenges that face the entirety of the plastics value chain," says Darroch. Sky Ocean Ventures has also partnered with Imperial College's Grantham Institute, working towards a common goal of protecting the environment by supporting promising business and exciting scientific innovations. "Internationally renowned academics and enthusiastic entrepreneurs from the Grantham Institute and its European network will explore solutions at all stages of the problem that sees more than five million tons of plastic enter the ocean each year," says Darroch.

So how is this done? Darroch says that Sky has thought long and hard about how to use innovation to change the world's plastic addiction and have decided to focus on disruptive technologies rather than projects that progress on a more incremental basis. "Our focus translates into new technologies across the plastics value chain, with new materials that can replace plastics from sustainable natural resource," says Darroch. "We are also exploring how to use digital tools to create more responsible consumption at both the consumer and business level. And finally we are looking hard at how circular-economy principles can be applied to plastics, where new science can improve the end-of-life treatment of the material."

Sky Ocean Ventures has so far invested in two companies that are focused on creating sustainable alternatives to plastic. Skipping Rocks Labs uses seaweed to create a natural and edible membrane that can encapsulate liquids in various formats to replace single-use plastics, and Choose Water is the first fully plastic-less water bottle. "We also have investments in the immediate pipeline around new material technologies and designs for a range of plastic use cases and also some specific software solutions that can improve the digitisation of how we collect, sort and recycle plastics," says Darroch.

Darroch emphasises that as well as equity investment, Sky can offer a range of services, infrastructure and mentoring for entrepreneurs. "We have set up a programme, Innovators in Residence, to trial products on Sky's West London campus," he says. "Each investee company is provided with the support of volunteer Sky executives to solve their hardest business problems, across all areas: including product, marketing, business strategy, operations and finance. Moreover, and most importantly, each innovative solution will also be showcased on Sky channels to raise awareness among our viewers, help adoption and change behaviours."
www.skyoceanventures.com

An Exmoor Pony grazing on North Berwick Law, one of the native breeds which are being promoted by Rare Breed Survival Trust

A breed apart

RARE BREEDS SURVIVAL TRUST

Rare Breeds Survival Trust promotes age-old livestock breeds that were nearly forced into extinction by intensive farming methods

Rare Breeds Survival Trust (RBST) is a charity that exists to conserve and promote native UK breeds of farm livestock. "It would be easy to question why something as apparently prolific as farm livestock should be in need of conservation, but the key is in the word native," says Chair of RBST Gail Sprake. "The breeds we focus on are those native breeds that for centuries fed, clothed and provided transport for every level of society. They evolved to thrive on whatever natural nutrition was available and their grazing habits helped shape the landscape on which they lived."

For over 30 years, RBST has benefited from the patronage of the Prince of Wales. "Our pedigree farm livestock is just as much a part of Britain's heritage as are her castles, her art collections and her historic churches," said His Royal Highness in a 1996 speech.

By the 1970s the heritage and diversity of native breeds was under threat. Farming practices were changing to meet the challenges of high-volume food production for growing populations. New generations of farmers moved away from traditional breeds in favour of those more suited to modern intensive methods, focusing on a narrow band of breeds that were seen to have greater commercial value. These trends brought the decline, in some cases to the point of extinction, of many native breeds. Happily, some people understood the heritage and the inherent genetic value of these breeds and saw a reason to ensure their future, and they became the founding force behind RBST.

In the early 1970s, when RBST was founded, the imperative for native breeds was survival. Flying in the face of farming fashion, dedicated enthusiasts took on breeds that commercial farmers had turned their backs on, and concentrated on maintaining and developing the bloodlines that gave each breed its strength and identity. Their aim wasn't to keep their animals as museum pieces. They recognised the role that these breeds had played in farming heritage but this was combined with an understanding of the importance of maintaining the genetic diversity that they represented.

"Today we have a clearer understanding of why that diversity matters," says Sprake. "Back in the 1970s, RBST's founders probably wouldn't have imagined the challenges that lay ahead. Back then, the world of farming was looking at a surplus of grain and it was a logical development to use it to feed intensively reared livestock. Today, questions are raised about the ethics of dedicating vast acres of crops to go for animal feed when we have a growing world population to feed."

Native breeds thrive on the landscape that they have helped to shape, often on marginal land that otherwise has no productive use. In fact, their grazing helps manage and sustain such land in the way that nature intended. The diversity of their genetics offers a resource the potential of which is yet to be fully explored.

Broadcaster and farmer, Jimmy Doherty, a zoology graduate, is President of RBST. "Through my academic studies, I developed an understanding of the ecological importance of a diversity of insects and plants," he says. "Without diversity, we don't have stability. We need the diversity that rare breeds represent. Today's generation needs to understand how relevant traditional breeds are to modern food production." *www.rbst.org.uk*

Horse power

BROOKE: ACTION FOR WORKING HORSES AND DONKEYS

Brooke: Action For Working Horses And
Donkeys works with communities around
the world who are reliant on beasts of burden

Left and right: *Brooke's support helps to empower women and men to strengthen their lives through the benefit of being a horse or donkey owner*

"If I don't have a donkey, I am the donkey." Those are the powerful words of just one of the women whose equine communities are supported by Brooke: Action For Working Horses & Donkeys. Horses, donkeys and mules are integral to the livelihoods of more than 600 million people in the developing world, and Brooke takes a development approach to their welfare.

"These working equines either relieve the family of household duties, or they're earning an income – which is often the only source of income for a family of six or more people," explains Brooke CEO Petra Ingram. "If the donkey or horse is not well, or dies, the family is plunged into even greater poverty. However, a lot of the welfare problems that we see can be easily prevented by better knowledge and understanding of the animals' needs."

Originally founded by Dorothy Brooke as The Old War Horse Memorial Hospital in Cairo, Egypt, in 1934, Brooke – whose vision is a world where working horses, donkeys and mules are free from suffering – today works in 11 countries across Africa, Asia, Latin America and the Middle East, and has now helped more than 2 million working equines. "Our strategy is focused on making lasting change, so we don't go in and relieve the suffering immediately ourselves," Ingram explains. "Instead, we build the capacity within the areas where the animals live, so there are people available locally to support them."

HRH The Duchess of Cornwall has been President of Brooke since 2006, after first witnessing the charity's work in the aftermath of the 2005 Pakistan earthquake. She's since seen first-hand how Brooke's work improves the lives of equine communities in Egypt, Jordan and India. Working with local vets, farriers and owners – as well as national and international policy-makers – Brooke seeks to ensure that those responsible for the equines' welfare have a full and proper understanding of how to look after their animal.

For Ingram, the most significant aspect of their work is the impact it has on women in the developing world. "When women don't have a donkey to help with their daily tasks, you see them carrying water on their heads, or firewood on their backs," she says. "I've even seen a woman pick up the shaft of a cart and pull it herself because her donkey had died. Women are often very vulnerable in communities, but if they know how to look after their animal and protect it as an asset, it can have a really dramatic impact on their lives."

In countries like Afghanistan and India, women are engaged to set up community support groups, where women can help other women. "It's quite humbling when you meet women who have built a support network for themselves and their animals," says Ingram. "They tend to all pay into a savings scheme, so if one of them has a problem – if their animal gets sick or dies – they can take a loan from their community fund."

In this way, Brooke helps empower women – and men – to strengthen their lives through the benefit of being a horse or donkey owner. "If something brings a value to the community, that value will be recognised," says Ingram. "So if somebody gets a benefit from their animal, they'll be more inclined to look after it. It's all about taking a holistic approach to create lasting change. If you improve the welfare of the animal, it will benefit the welfare of people in those communities. Having an animal that's fit and well really does keep people out of poverty." *www.thebrooke.org*

CHAPTER TWELVE

Sustainable fashion and fabrics

Smart materials

The market might be dominated by artificial fibres made from fossil fuels, but the world is slowly waking up to the beauty and practicality of eco-friendly natural fabrics such as wool, cotton and linen

The fabric of life

MAKING A MATERIAL CHANGE

The Prince of Wales has tirelessly raised awareness
of the importance and value of sustainable,
natural materials

"Wool, as I never tire of pointing out, is not only one of the oldest fibres known to mankind, it is also one of the most beneficial," said the Prince of Wales in a reception for the Campaign For Wool at Clarence House in 2014. "But, during the 20th century, we have lost sight of the long-term value of Nature and her genius. It is perhaps a sobering thought that only 1.3 per cent of clothes today are made from wool, whereas 60 per cent are made from synthetic materials."

Prince Charles has long supported the use of sustainable fibres and naturally sourced fabrics. "As someone who minds deeply about the prospects for farmers and rural livelihoods and worries about the desperate environmental consequences for our children and grandchildren of relying on products made from fossil fuels, this is a cause that means a lot to me," he said. "We will discover that wool does no damage to the Earth, simply replenishes it, whereas the masses of synthetic material we put in the ground simply stays there and then eventually leeches many damaging chemicals."

So alarmed was the Prince about the decline of wool as a fabric of choice among manufacturers, and the low prices that farmers were receiving for their wool, that he convened a group of representatives from the farming, fashion and interior design industries to see what could be done. The result was an organisation called the Campaign For Wool, formed on a freezing cold morning in January 2010. "It was in an unbelievably cold barn on National Trust property," recalls the Prince. "I don't think I've ever been so cold in my life, but it did actually require a lot of wool!"

In the intervening eight years, the campaign has successfully fulfilled many of its objectives. "We wanted to ensure a sustainable supply of wool from across the Commonwealth and beyond," said the Prince in a 2016 speech at Dumfries House. "And to do that we knew we would have to raise awareness amongst consumers about the unique benefits offered by wool and draw attention to the ecological advantages it delivers." To this end the campaign put together the Dumfries House Wool Declaration in September 2016, listing 10 indisputable truths about wool: that wool is 100 per cent natural, renewable, biodegradable, odour-resistant, fire-resistant and fire-retardant, welfare assured, part of a natural carbon cycle, a natural alternative to wasteful consumer practices and improves indoor air quality.

The campaign united wool farmers from all over the Commonwealth. "One of the great successes of the campaign has been the way in which four previously rival wool organisations – representing the UK, Australia, South Africa and New Zealand – came together under the umbrella of the Campaign For Wool," said the Prince in 2016. "We are no longer faced with the crazy situation whereby farmers were being paid less for a fleece than the cost of shearing it, which was very much the reality, I can assure you, when I convened this campaign. That is why I brought together wool interests, wool organisations and the fashion sector to encourage them to work together for a better economic landscape and common benefit.

"Since my campaign was launched, the price of wool has tripled, which means that farmers and wool growers in this country, and across the Commonwealth, are receiving a little more than they were for their wool, which might thus enable farmers and rural communities to remain doing what they do so well, helping to maintain the countryside we take for granted."

Opposite: *Prince of Wales visits the MYB Lace Factory in Newmilns, Scotland, July 2014*

Nature's miracle fibre

THE WOOLMARK COMPANY

The global authority on Merino wool, Australia's
The Woolmark Company shares Prince Charles's
enthusiasm for wool as a fabric for the future

"Imagine the excitement if a new fibre were to be invented with a seemingly miraculous range of properties," said the Prince of Wales in a 2016 speech. The miraculous fibre in question was, of course, natural, renewable, biodegradable wool.

"Turning our backs on wool – the most versatile of natural fibres, used successfully since medieval times – in favour of synthetics, seemed short-sighted in the extreme," said the Prince. "Natural materials that do not require fossil fuels to make them and that can be recycled endlessly are going to be more important than ever as we face up to the challenges of climate change." He even set fire to two garments – one synthetic, the other wool – proving that the woollen garment was more fire resistant, and buried a polyester sweater and a woollen one in the grounds of Clarence House. When he revisited them five months later the synthetic sweater was intact, while the woollen one had "quietly and usefully biodegraded itself away to nothing".

It's a stance towards woollen clothing that is wholeheartedly supported by The Woolmark Company, an organisation based in Sydney, Australia. As the global authority on wool, The Woolmark Company works with textile and fashion industries at every level, developing better wool textiles and driving consumer demand.

"I have been fortunate to have met the Prince on a couple of occasions and I cannot speak highly enough of him and the work that he has done for the wool industry," says Stuart McCullough, Managing Director of The Woolmark Company. "He has made it one of his many missions to show the sustainability of wool on his travels and has always done his best to support the farmers, suppliers indeed all aspects of the industry. He has always had the vision on these

bigger issues – such as the way plastics are polluting our oceans and getting into the food chain."

The Woolmark Company is a subsidiary of Australian Wool Innovation, a not-for-profit enterprise that conducts research, development and marketing along the worldwide supply chain for Australian wool on behalf of 60,000 farmers that help fund the company. Through its extensive network of relationships spanning the global textile and fashion industries, The Woolmark Company highlights Australian wool's position as the ultimate natural fibre and premier ingredient in luxury apparel. The Woolmark logo – born in 1964 – is one of the world's most recognised and respected brands, an independent quality assurance of every wool product it adorns – more than five billion of them.

Merino sheep have been a vital part of Australian farming for more than 200 years, and The Woolmark Company has been instrumental in the development and promotion of Merino wool products. Odour resistant, breathable and having excellent moisture management, it is ideal for sports and physical activity, but it is also fine and soft enough to be perfect for haute couture. Innovations can be introduced into Merino wool at any stage in the manufacturing process, making it a versatile and cutting-edge alternative to other fibres.

"The new generation of consumers across the world are discerning about fabric," says McCullough. "They want to know where the product has come from and believe in it being energy efficient and sustainable, as it matters to them. We at The Woolmark Company are delighted to be part of this celebratory publication and are happy to acknowledge the Prince's work, particularly his great support to the wool industry."
www.woolmark.com

Hebridean heritage

HARRIS TWEED HEBRIDES

Harris Tweed Hebrides focuses on traditional textile production methods to produce a unique handwoven woollen fabric, recognised by the famous "Orb" certification mark

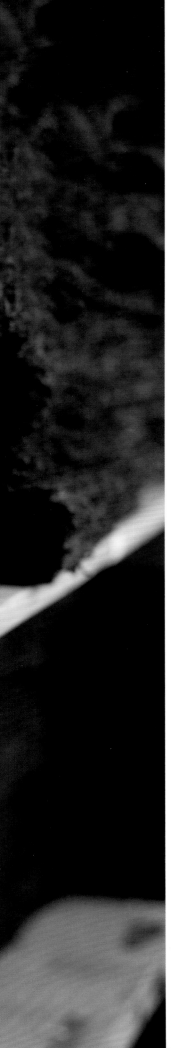

Left: *Made on the Scottish island of Lewis and Haris, Harris Tweed Hebrides is now a fixture on high-fashion catwalks globally*

Right: *Ian Taylor of Harris Tweed Hebrides*

"When in Scotland, Prince Charles's title is the Duke of Rothesay," says Ian Angus Mackenzie, Chief Executive of Harris Tweed Hebrides. "He also has the title Lord of the Isles, something he is clearly mindful of. He is passionate about his support of Hebridean culture and the unique Harris Tweed industry. Whenever he is here he makes a point of wearing his Harris Tweed jacket and tartan kilt. I know supporting the indigenous tweed industry is very important to him."

It's not just royalty who wear Harris Tweed Hebrides fabric. Today, the classic fabric is widely seen on men's and ladies' jackets on the fashion catwalks of New York, Paris and Milan, and is also used in bags, hats, scarves, shoes and even furniture around the world. But only a few years ago, the industry – with more than a century of history – was at a low ebb, to the point where its future was in jeopardy.

"A decade ago, Shawbost Mill on the Isle of Lewis was closed and derelict," says Mackenzie. "We refurbished the mill, re-established production and now employ more than 80 staff, as well as providing year-round work for more than 120 Harris Tweed weavers who weave each and every metre of fabric from their croft homes located across the island of Lewis and Harris."

Mackenzie, an expert in the industry, teamed up with London-based businessman Ian Taylor, and former Labour MP and Trade Minister Brian Wilson to form the company. It is now responsible for 75 per cent of all Harris Tweed production. The UK is the largest market for sales, but the company also exports to more than 50 different countries including Japan, Italy, Germany, the United States and South Korea.

From the outset, the company worked to reposition Harris Tweed as a forward-facing fashion fabric, and it is now regularly used in the fashion collections of such global brands as Prada, Yves Saint Laurent, Manolo Blahnik and Vivienne Westwood, who work with the Shawbost-based design team.

As well as apparel, Harris Tweed Hebrides has expanded by moving into interiors. "One of our key accounts in recent years has been the Preston-based furniture manufacturer Tetrad," says Mackenzie. "Tetrad makes high-quality furniture in the UK using Harris Tweed fabric as a focus for its collection."

Harris Tweed is uniquely protected by the Harris Tweed Act of 1993, and the famous "Orb" certification mark, which requires the entire manufacturing process to be undertaken within the Outer Hebrides. Harris Tweed Hebrides has won numerous industry awards, including UK Textile Brand of the Year at the UK Fashion and Textile Awards in 2013 and Scottish Exporter of the Year in 2015. It has also been recognised by Investors in Young People for its investment in training, with a third of the company's workforce under 30 years of age.

"I have met Prince Charles on a number of occasions and been a guest of his at Dumfries House," says Ian Taylor, the company's principal investor. "He shares many of our core beliefs at Harris Tweed Hebrides. He takes heritage seriously and believes in the importance of genuine, original products. Like us he believes in sustainable business and supporting the local community. He is, of course, passionate about the use of natural, sustainable fabrics and has been a key player in the Campaign for Wool. He has been a great supporter of our industry, and everyone at Harris Tweed Hebrides wishes him a very happy 70th birthday and many happy returns."
www.harristweedhebrides.com

Change for good

TEXTILE EXCHANGE & THE 2025 SUSTAINABLE COTTON CHALLENGE

In collaboration with leading brands and retailers, Textile Exchange is helping the Prince of Wales to promote sustainable, fairly traded cotton farming

"The Prince of Wales has been able to place the issues that come with conventionally grown cotton on the global stage," says La Rhea Pepper. "He has moved the industry from token programmes of organic and fairly traded cotton to making long-term commitments. This created a critical mass across a number of more sustainable, organic and Fair Trade initiatives and allowed His Royal Highness to influence more than a dozen brands – including M&S, Nike, Burberry and Ikea – to make a public commitment and to annually report their use of more sustainably grown cotton."

La Rhea Pepper, Managing Director of Textile Exchange, grew up on a cotton farm. She and her husband started farming in 1979 and became one of the first cotton farms to be certified organic in 1990. When the Prince Of Wales's International Sustainability Unit was looking for industry support to promote sustainable cotton farming, Textile Exchange, an organisation founded by Pepper in 2002, was a natural fit to promote the use of more sustainable cotton among brands.

Textile Exchange's initiative the 2025 Sustainable Cotton Challenge is gaining momentum. When the challenge was launched in May 2017, 13 brands pledged to use 100 per cent sustainable cotton by 2025. A year later, that number had swelled to more than 40 major brands with additional brands joining the challenge. When the International Sustainability Unit closed in March 2018, responsibility for the initiative was handed to Textile Exchange. A steering committee with representatives from Soil Association, Marks & Spencer, Levi Strauss & Co, Kering, Better Cotton Initiative, and Textile Exchange guide this work and generate an annual report.

"It's all about supporting more responsible choices for brands and giving consumers that choice as well," says Pepper. The sustainable approach benefits both people and the planet. Organic and regenerative farming improves biodiversity and the ecosystem, and it also has tangible material advantages. "It changes the socioeconomic dynamics because the farmers get a fair price and are no longer dependent on one crop, because the organic system requires crop rotation," she explains. "We're not just reducing pesticides and other toxic chemicals, it goes deeper than that. It's about connected action – an industry working together to create positive change."

As part of its wider work, Textile Exchange builds integrity by providing chain-of-custody standards for several fibres and materials including the Responsible Wool Standard, Responsible Down Standard, Global Recycled Standard and Organic Content Standard. Textile Exchange also creates and commissions reports and encourages brands to support their peers in providing best practise.

"The intention is to go beyond sustainable," says Pepper. "We want to integrate best practices in agriculture that will actively improve lives rather than maintain the status quo. We want to create healthy and resilient communities where the cotton is grown so that it becomes a positive tool. There's a lot of opportunity to do good. Now brands no longer have a token sustainability programme, they are adopting a proactive strategy for their cotton use. It's been very exciting to witness the Prince of Wales using his influence to protect and promote cotton as a tool for positive change."
textileexchange.org

Textile Exchange recognises that employing a sustainable approach to cotton production actively improves lives

Covering the world

CAMIRA FABRICS

From its home in Huddersfield, West Yorkshire, the award-winning Camira Fabrics is exporting its sustainable and eco-friendly materials around the world

Anyone who works in an office, spends time in a hotel, sits in a university lecture theatre, or travels by bus, coach or train will almost certainly have encountered one of the many hundreds of upholstery materials produced by Camira. "You're sure to have touched upon our fabrics either at work, at play or on the move," says Ian Burn, the company's Director of Marketing.

From design through to production and distribution, Camira controls the entire process of the 8 million metres of fabric it makes every year. It employs 750 people globally and operates some 100 looms across 500,000 sq ft of manufacturing space in the UK and Lithuania.

Its capability starts with the yarn itself, from wool spinning and polypropylene yarn manufacture, through to yarn dyeing, warping, weaving, technical knitting and textile finishing. This means that Camira can ensure continuity of supply and quality excellence for its customers far and wide. "We are very privileged to be able to manufacture all our fabrics ourselves," says Burn, "going right from the farm to the fabric and handling everything in between."

Camira exports around two thirds of its output to overseas markets in mainland Europe, North America, Asia and Australasia, but is a proudly British company. It has been based near Huddersfield in West Yorkshire since 1974 but, through a series of acquisitions, its history can be traced back to 1783.

As well as delivering commercial success, for the past two decades the company has pioneer°ed innovations in sustainable development of fabrics as part of a mission to reduce its environmental impact. It was one of the first recipients of the ISO 14001 environmental management systems standard. "Sustainability is our warp and weft," says Burn. "It's within the very fibres of Camira and at the heart of our culture and ethos."

The firm collaborated with De Montfort University and the UK's Department for Environment, Food and Rural Affairs in a groundbreaking project to blend virgin wool with harvested nettles. The project, known as STING (Sustainable Technology in Nettle Growing), discovered that the blend was naturally fire retardant and it is now found in the company's Nettle Collection of textile patterns. The same safety benefit emerged from blends of wool and hemp, and wool and flax. Camira Fabrics has also devised methods to use recycled polyester from plastic bottles and post-industrial materials to make more sustainable fabrics.

These achievements helped secure two Queen's Award for Sustainable Development accolades, presented in 2010 and 2015, with the most recent bestowed for five years of continuous environmental improvement and best-in-class performance. Camira has won three other Queen's Awards. In 2016 it secured the International Trade Award, which it also received in 1997 in recognition of its export achievements. In 2005 it received the Innovation Award, putting the fabric industry on a par with science and engineering.

The company, which is set to post a turnover of almost £100 million in 2018, has further ambitious growth plans which it is targeting through both market development and product innovation. "We want to elevate the profile of Camira and are looking at the markets that will help achieve this," says Burn. "We are very proud of our British roots, our global position and the fact that we are making a positive difference."
www.camirafabrics.com

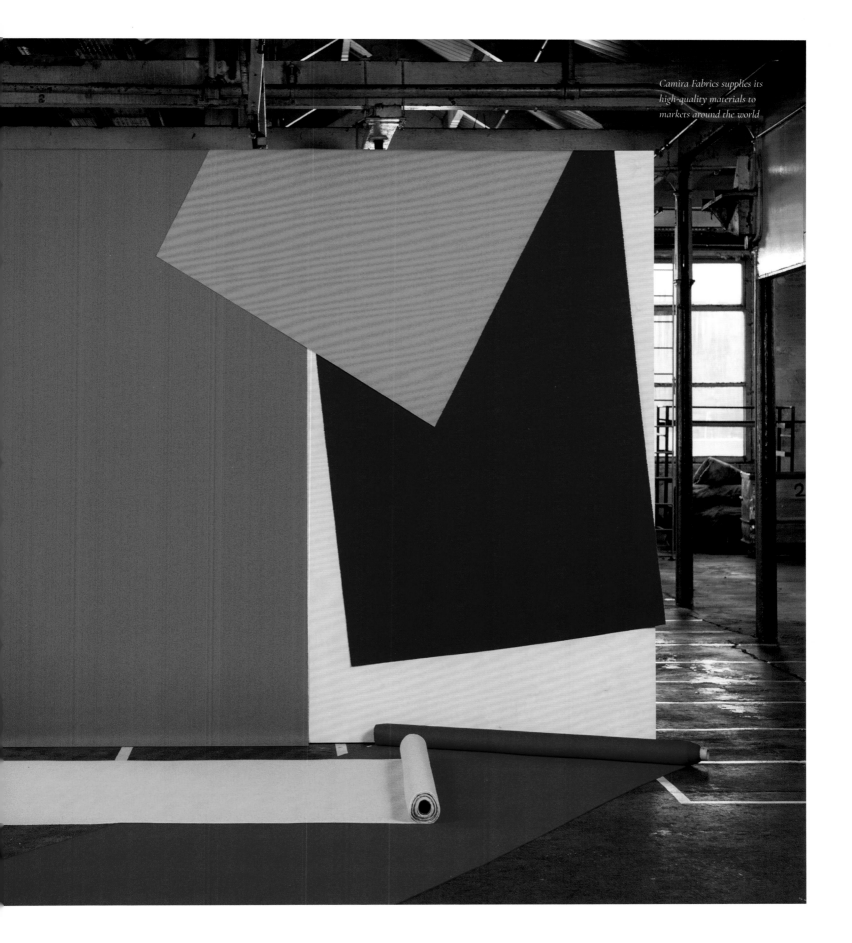

Camira Fabrics supplies its high-quality materials to markets around the world

CHAPTER THIRTEEN

Captain of industry
Responsible business

The most successful global businesses have been making a commitment to sustainability, the environment and corporate social responsibility

A wealth of ideas

INVESTING IN THE FUTURE

The first royal to enter industry himself, Prince Charles speaks about corporate responsibility and environmentally conscious business from a position of knowledge

Having served as the President of his charity Business in the Community for more than a quarter of a century, Prince Charles has spent considerable time among industry leaders. As a result, he has been able to both absorb and share knowledge and opinions regarding industry, and particularly his own commitment to sustainable industry. The Prince is one of the few members of the Royal Family to have ventured into industry himself, having created the Duchy Originals brand, selling organic food and drink and using the profits to support his charities. He has put his principles into practice, and reaped the rewards. He has also taken his message directly to business leaders and industries throughout the world, talking to business school and economic forums about the role capital investment can play in improving the planet.

Business in the Community is one of several initiatives supported by the Prince in this area. It is a business-led membership organisation made up of progressive businesses of all sizes who understand that the prosperity of business and society are mutually dependent. This aligns with the Prince's long-term thinking about commerce and industry, which has seen him insist companies can behave responsibly while remaining profitable. "The message at the heart of Business in the Community is very simple," he has said. "The prosperity of business and society and the whole of the natural environment on which we depend for our ultimate survival, are intimately tied together."

Time after time, Prince Charles has driven this message home. "We need our economy – and the businesses which operate in it – to think about their inherent resilience, by which I mean their ability to absorb, adapt or repel exogenous shocks," he said in a speech to the London Business School in 2011. The Prince then called for "partnerships between the public and private sectors in such a way that they have, built into them, the necessary flexibility that can adapt to rapidly altering

circumstances. Capitalism depends upon capital, but our capital ultimately depends upon the health of Nature's capital. Whether we like it or not, the two are in fact inseparable."

The Prince's advocacy of responsibility in business has been numerous major manufacturers respond positively to his message. This is because the Prince has always argued that the solutions to the world's environmental challenges lies with businesses – they have the creativity, imagination, power and wealth to help transform the planet in a positive fashion.

As he told the Commonwealth Business Forum in Malta in 2015, "the private sector is absolutely critical". At the London Business School the same year he expanded on this theme: "It seems clear to me that those who find ways to use natural resources in a sustainable, and 'circular' way, with nothing going to waste, will find themselves uncovering new sources of innovation, reducing their risks and increasing their competitive advantage. Even more, success will be defined by those who have shown real leadership in helping us to change trajectory and avoid the worst outcomes that, at present, seem so likely."

To support his arguments, His Royal Highness has created several initiatives, such as his Accounting for Sustainability Project, ClimateWise, the Banking Environment Initiative and the Investment Leaders Group, all of which have been designed to work with the research, finance and accounting communities to support a fundamental shift towards business models that drive a sustainable economy. These initiatives have worked with world-leading multinational companies, united by a determination to find environmental solutions that offer economic benefits. "We can only achieve the transformation we need by encouraging enlightened business leadership to see its relationship with society as a mutually beneficial partnership," he says. "And nurturing a more balanced, more dynamic and much more sustainable economy in the future."

Below: *The Prince Of Wales hosts a reception at Clarence House in September 2013, celebrating the 21st anniversary of his Duchy Originals brand*

Below: *"We are already one of the world's most CO2-efficient steel companies," says Bimlendra Jha, "but we want to go further"*

Sustainable steel

TATA STEEL

In setting up the Industrial Cadets programme, global steel giant Tata Steel helped to fulfil Prince Charles's wish to inspire a new generation

Prince Charles was on his third visit to Tata Steel's Port Talbot works in Wales when he joked that every time he came, he saw photos of himself on previous tours "getting more decrepit" each time. On that occasion in 2012, His Royal Highness was at Port Talbot to see the rebuilding of the No 4 Blast Furnace at the steelworks which had originally opened following a royal visit from the Prince's parents in the 1960s.

Tata Steel, one of Europe's largest steel producers, has a strong commitment to sustainability, innovation and community. These are interests that are shared by Prince Charles, so it's fitting the three strands came together with the creation of Industrial Cadets, an education programme designed to introduce young people at schools and universities to the workplace, where they could join Tata Steel and other companies in developing new and exciting technologies to improve sustainability.

Industrial Cadets was created following conversations with the Prince of Wales when he visited a Tata Steel site in the north east, and Charles launched the national initiative in January 2013. "When an employment-oriented initiative has the backing of the future King, Tata Steel was obviously delighted to take the lead in developing and shaping it," says Bimlendra Jha, CEO of Tata Steel UK.

Sustainability, in every sense of the word, is an important concern for both Tata Steel and the Prince of Wales. Integrated steelmaking in Port Talbot, stretching back more than a century, has acted as an anchor to socio-economic sustainability in Wales as in other parts of UK and the Netherlands, providing not just support in the form of highly skilled jobs for generations, but a positive financial impact on the surrounding area and a boost for the many other businesses which have links to the steelworks.

"An integrated steel plant is a microcosm of a circular economy," says Jha. "Most of its solid, liquid, gaseous waste and heat are reused for producing useful products such as aromatics and electricity. We are now extending the idea to link the waste cycle of other industries by supporting research at the universities of Swansea and Warwick as well as our own R&D."

The challenge of environmental sustainability, however, is growing by the size of demand. Economic prosperity and demand for better quality of life has increased consumption of materials at an unprecedented scale, leaving a life-threatening carbon footprint. The steel industry thus needs to rise to the challenge and lead the way towards a carbon-neutral world.

"Tata Steel is already one of the world's most CO_2-efficient steel companies, but we want to go further," says Jha. "Our goal is to be carbon neutral from 2050. We will develop and nurture innovations which have the potential to change the way steel is produced." Green shoots are already visible with breakthrough innovations such as Hisarna – a new technology which Tata Steel developed to drastically reduce carbon emissions. The company has recently announced partnerships to produce naphtha from carbon monoxide – a byproduct gas from blast furnaces.

"We are a vital link in the circular economy," says Jha. "An integrated steel plant has the unique ability to recycle societal waste and steel scrap. However, there is always a demand for new steel which out-strips the amount of scrap which can be recycled." Steel is never "consumed" – once made, it is used again and again without loss of quality or strength, making it the world's most recycled material. Tata Steel is known for its steel production from virgin ores, but it remains the UK's largest steel recycler.
www.tatasteeleurope.com

Steeling beauty

ALL STEELS TRADING LIMITED

Based in North Yorkshire but active globally,
All Steels Trading is an enthusiastic Patron
of The Prince's Trust

Opposite: Sustainability is a key issue for All Steels Trading, as is giving back to the local community

Anyone who has seen a building site knows what steel is. Few people outside the industry would be familiar, however, with the sorts of specialist steels required for the transmission tower or automotive industries. Premier bulk steel firm All Steels Trading, which is based in North Yorkshire, is one of Europe's fastest growing steel-trading companies due in large part to its skill in sourcing niche steel supplies from trusted mills worldwide.

All Steels Trading was incorporated in 2006, but before that its Managing Director Laurence McDougall had built up some 20 years of industry experience and expertise. While All Steels Trading is a bulk trader that imports and exports an extensive range of general construction steels, it differentiates itself from the competition in its ability to source and supply a range of speciality steels. It can, for instance, quickly source and supply high-yield steels for the offshore industry as well as micro-alloy grades such as boron steel for hot forging.

The business relies on strong international trading relationships with mills that meet rigorous standards of quality, reliability and sustainability. "Having a multilingual workforce sharpens All Steels Trading's competitive edge in the global arena," says McDougall. "We embrace and value the diversity of thoughts, ideas and ways of working that people from different backgrounds bring to our organisation."

Purchases from Turkish mills account for 35 per cent of All Steels Trading's commerce. Recognising that mills in Turkey tend to be fitted with the latest technology and operated 24 hours a day by a young, educated workforce, McDougall has partnered with select mills from whom he has been able to order niche products. At the same time, he has helped the mills commercialise their expanded product range.

Sustainable production is an important criterion when selecting steel mills. "We primarily purchase steel from mills that operate electric arc furnaces," says McDougall. "Such furnaces typically produce new steel products from scrap steel using 75 per cent less energy than furnaces used in ore-based steel production." All Steels Trading ensures that the mills from which it sources are fully certified and that materials are all CE (Conformité Européene) marked. All Steels Trading itself carries the prestigious British Standards Institution ISO 9001:2015 certification.

From its warehouses based on the River Trent off the Humber Estuary, All Steels Trading operates from a highly efficient 12-berth port-side facility. Its extensive warehousing is equipped with the latest remote-control cranes and has access to a streamlined logistics service. Warehouse management and deliveries are outsourced to Groveport Logistics, allowing All Steels Trading to concentrate on providing sourcing solutions to its customers.

As the company has grown, so has its opportunity to give back to the local community. As a Patron of The Prince's Trust, All Steels Trading supports vulnerable young people who need help stabilising their lives. "It's ingenious the way that The Prince's Trust has changed young people's lives, not through condescension and free hand-outs, but by giving them the means to help themselves," says McDougall. "Members of our team enjoy taking part in fundraising events and working directly with young people on voluntary programmes to further support the charity."

Helping the next generation of workers find its feet while increasing current local employment are the bonuses of this fast-expanding business for McDougall. "It's extremely pleasing to trade internationally in a material that genuinely contributes to environmental, economic and societal sustainability," he says. "Steel is vital to achieving the needs of today without impacting society's ability to meet the needs of the future."
www.allsteelstrading.co.uk

Patent perfection

MINESOFT

Minesoft's search systems help businesses around the world navigate the complicated world of intellectual property

Innovation would not be shared so widely in business without the security offered by patents. The British company Minesoft helps businesses around the world to navigate the complex world of intellectual property with its sophisticated patent-search system, PatBase.

"Anyone can use a patent that's expired," explains Ann Chapman, who founded the company with her husband Ophir Daniel. "Our sophisticated research tools mean they can find an existing technical solution then develop it for another use. The defence industry, for example, has created coatings for spy planes that deflect light and radiation. This makes them ideal also for painting on buildings or road surfaces in hot parts of the world to reduce temperatures and the effects of climate change."

Since 2000, Minesoft has been developing solutions which assist innovation across the world. Ninety per cent of its business is from outside the UK, including emerging markets such as India and African countries. In recognition of its achievements, Minesoft won a Queen's Award for International Trade in 2009 and again in 2015.

What began around the kitchen table has grown into a global business employing 60 staff, with its headquarters in Richmond, Surrey. A key part of Minesoft's work is sending staff out to developing nations, including many in the Commonwealth. With the aim of fostering positive change, this initiative teaches them how to use the company's specialist research tools. This is often through free or low-cost access which has been made possible through a public-private partnership involving the World Intellectual Property Organization (WIPO) and leading patent information providers.

To enable customers to access the most current information, PatBase is updated every day and provides a resource of millions of patent documents. A recent development has been a more powerful search system for the database. One benefit is that hidden patents, which previously may have been missed with regular keyword searches, can now be unearthed. Chemical-structure searches are also possible via text-mining algorithms.

Minesoft has also been working closely with large corporations to create Pat-KM, a product offering customised database and archives. "Customers can access a central location where they can monitor, search and share patent information – and be ahead in their field," says Chapman. "Again, this is very much a global product with innovators looking to monitor what has been successful in their region."

One example is of Malaysia's expanding expertise in pharmaceuticals. "We feed companies data about what others are doing," says Chapman. "They are notified quickly about any new entrants developing technology similar to theirs, and about licensing opportunities. R&D in new development areas can cost millions. But this way they often come across groups of researchers who can share expertise and help them generate new ideas around their products."

With leading corporations, patent offices and law firms among its customers, Minesoft has come a long way from its humble beginnings. It has achieved this without taking on outside investment but instead in always being forward thinking in growing the company's network and locating new partners. "Often people go out and spread the word for us about our area of expertise," says Chapman.

Just as it enables others to breathe new life into what already exists, Minesoft is committed to progressing by building on its own firm foundations. And as this company's products demonstrate, it is always possible to teach new tricks to those willing to learn.
www.minesoft.com

Below: *With the very international Minesoft team – drawn from 16 different countries – at home on Richmond Green*

Below: *"We drive brands to achieve their full potential," says Edwin Bessant, Ceuta Group's Chief Executive, pictured with co-founder Annette D'Abreo*

Global brand outsourcing

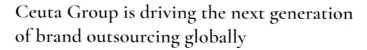

CEUTA GROUP

Ceuta Group is driving the next generation of brand outsourcing globally

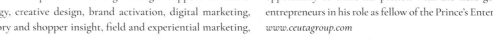

Edwin Bessant, Chief Executive of Ceuta Group, believes true business acumen is being able to think ahead. But when he and joint-founding partner Annette D'Abreo took a leap of faith, leaving aspiring careers at US healthcare giant Pfizer behind to start out on their own, even they didn't expect the business they created to be the global success it is today.

Bessant had been on Pfizer's fast-track programme, heading straight for the very top levels of the company. But, after assessing the UK healthcare market in the early 1990s, he discovered a gap in the market with companies wanting an alternative and more affordable solution to calling on pharmacies. Bessant and D'Abreo seized the opportunity and, with just five employees in 1994, Ceuta Healthcare was born, providing outsourced sales solutions, training and in-store category planning for health and personal care brands. Soon the operation grew to become a sought-after service for brand owners, from large multinationals to start-ups. It also expanded internationally, supporting brands across Europe, Asia, North America and the Middle East.

"I noticed over time that brand owners were struggling to bring external agencies together to work on specific projects to manage and grow their brands," says Bessant. "This became the catalyst for expanding our offering and forming Ceuta Group."

From there, Bessant embarked on a strategic acquisition strategy, adding a collection of brand specialist businesses to his portfolio, delivering their services through a single, integrated platform; supporting the journey of a brand from concept to execution; allowing Ceuta Group to deliver everything a brand owner would ever want or need from one outsourced partner.

Today, Ceuta Group comprises 12 consumer brand specialist companies delivering strategic support in brand strategy, creative design, brand activation, digital marketing, category and shopper insight, field and experiential marketing,

data analytics, logistics and go-to-market sales and marketing to over 250 clients in more than 100 international markets.

Ceuta Group offers a complete outsourced brand-management solution known as "Brand Fostering" as well as a tailored combination of specialist brand services that perfectly match the needs of their clients on a global footprint. This model is appealing to both manufacturers and private equity companies who acquire brands but don't want bricks and mortar, but want to retain the intellectual property.

"We are seeing a market where companies are looking for global solutions," says Bessant, "but they want to work with a partner who can provide stability, continuity and the same standard of performance across the globe whilst also being financially sound, having outstanding values and supporting a strong corporate social responsibility agenda. That's exactly what we offer and, more importantly, what we deliver."

Bessant always keeps an eye on the market and looks three years ahead to ensure the ongoing success of Ceuta Group. "It is crucial to understand the traits of futurism around technology and operational advancements as well as evolving consumer needs and behaviours, as these changes can directly and indirectly change your business positioning and direction," he says. "There is also no point in taking your business forward if you don't take your people with you. Our people and our values have been the backbone of our business from day one, allowing us to develop a winning culture based on our passion for the brands we support and our commitment to achieving the best for our clients."

Bessant has achieved great success but never misses an opportunity to share his passion with the next generation of entrepreneurs in his role as fellow of the Prince's Enterprise Trust. *www.ceutagroup.com*

"Like everybody who lives in the United Arab Emirates, I believe in the growth of the country and in peace, safety and security," says Khalaf Ahmad Al Habtoor

Building prosperity

AL HABTOOR GROUP

As its links with the Royal Family and the UK illustrate, the Al Habtoor Group is a UAE firm with a thriving international outlook

He may be the founder of one of the most successful and respected conglomerates in the Gulf region, but Khalaf Ahmad Al Habtoor – Chairman of the Al Habtoor Group – also has a great love and affinity for the UK and its Royal Family.

Al Habtoor has written tributes to Her Majesty the Queen, whom he admires greatly and has met several times, both at charity dinners and during the annual Al Habtoor Royal Windsor Cup polo challenge, which takes place at the Guards Polo Club in Windsor Great Park. The Al Habtoor Group sponsored the tournament for five years and Al Habtoor's son Rashid has played polo with Prince Charles. The family's enthusiasm for the game led to the creation of the Al Habtoor Polo Resort in Dubai, a luxury resort surrounded by world-class polo fields, with stables housing as many as 550 horses. The Dubai-based polo team has since played with Princes William and Harry.

"It was an honour to be with Her Majesty and to meet Prince Philip too," says Al Habtoor. "A long time ago – in the '80s – I hosted Her Royal Highness Princess Anne for the horse show in Dubai. She then invited me to come to London. We had a great time. We now consider the United Kingdom to be our second home and we have a country house in Buckinghamshire, which is a beautiful area. We go there every summer, with the family."

The Al Habtoor Group started as a small Dubai-based engineering firm in 1970. It has since grown exponentially and now employs thousands of people all over the world, including in the US, Europe and Lebanon. Although the company straddles many industries – with interests in the hospitality, automotive, car leasing, real estate, education and publishing sectors – Al Habtoor says the group is currently focusing on its work in hospitality and real estate.

The almost-completed Al Habtoor City project – a multi-use development consisting of three hotels and residential towers, with restaurants and leisure facilities – has just won the top prize in the residential and hospitality category at the Engineering News-Record (ENR) Global Best Projects Competition 2018.

"The number of people who are going to live in this complex, at any one time, will be over 22,000," says Khalaf. "It's like a village – a town even – in the heart of Dubai. It is both luxurious and very important. I call Dubai, which is halfway between Asia and the West, the land of opportunity and the safe haven of the world. It's also a jewel, with people of every nationality living here in harmony."

Being a successful business is only part of the Al Habtoor Group's legacy. It is also highly focused on philanthropy, supporting charitable projects around the world. Al Habtoor believes in the right of all people to live a decent life, independent of race, religion or geography, and he says he finds serenity through giving and sharing what he has. Among other projects, he has worked with President Carter and the United Nations, and last year helped to set up food banks in Springfield, Illinois in the US.

Once Al Habtoor City is completed, Al Habtoor says the group is looking to expand overseas. But his heart will always lie with his homeland. "Like everybody else who lives in the United Arab Emirates, I believe in the growth of the country and in peace, safety and security," he says. "Whether visitor, resident or citizen, we in the UAE are all one family. I am proud of my country and I am pleased to represent it wherever I go."

www.habtoor.com

CHAPTER FOURTEEN

Iconic style
For the love of arts and crafts

From flawless fashion to fine art to handcrafted jewellery, the Prince of Wales has championed craftsmanship in all of its forms

A cut above

TIMELESS STYLE

A smart dresser, a keen painter and a passionate fan of craftsmanship, Prince Charles has established himself as a global style icon

When Prince Charles was named best dressed man of 2012 by *GQ* magazine, he confessed it came as a "complete surprise" to him. But perhaps it shouldn't have been such a shock. His Royal Highness has always epitomised what he describes as "the classic and timeless look of British style" through his favouring of elegant but hard-wearing handmade suits on Savile Row. But His Royal Highness's commitment to being a style icon is about more than just fashion. It chimes with some of his most passionate beliefs regarding craft and sustainability – views that were once seen as old-fashioned but which are now widely shared by the trendiest craftspeople, activists, artists and entrepreneurs around the country.

Prince Charles has always been both a connoisseur and patron of British menswear, most notably through wearing shoes, shirts and suits made by British craftsmen. Much of his life is spent at official functions, so for Prince Charles the handmade suit is a necessity as much as a sartorial decision. "Clothes have to combine style with sustainability," he said on receiving the GQ award, "and I find British-made tailoring more than meets that challenge." As he pointed out, his job requires him to wear clothes that can withstand a "heavy battering" and will "look as good at the end of a day as it did at the start", and this often means those that are made by skilled, trained craftsman using traditional materials such as wool, silk and cotton.

As such, the Prince's wardrobe aligns with his long-held and deeply felt commitments to craft and the environment. Prince Charles has been a firm advocate for the importance of retaining traditional artisan skills such as stonemasonry and carpentry. "Traditional crafts are as much a part of our shared heritage as our wonderful historic landscapes, beautiful buildings, rare breeds of native farm animals and varied museum collections," he has said. "I urgently believe that we must gather more information on the crafts identified so far to ensure that no more treasured skills are lost forever."

The Prince believes that these crafts aren't simply desirable in themselves, but that they are beneficial for the environment. He argues that traditional crafts are more sustainable than modern production methods because "with the acquisition of such skills comes a real enthusiasm for the natural materials with which these trades work".

This is a philosophy that Charles explored in more detail for his 2010 book *Harmony*, which demonstrated the way the Prince's commitment to craft and the environment corresponded with his strong personal style, whether applied to fashion, architecture or art. In the past, he has outlined his principles for architecture and has developed his own town at Poundbury in Dorset, which fuses traditional concepts of architecture with sustainable contemporary living and has proved incredibly popular with residents. The Prince is also a strong patron of the arts and enjoys painting himself; since 1992, sales of these have raised more than £2 million, money that goes towards his many charitable enterprises.

For the Prince, craft, style and sustainability are all interconnected, which explains why he has come to be seen as such an iconic figure. He firmly supports those "schemes [which] guarantee that the highest standards of British craftsmanship are in safe hands and are being passed on to the next generation." After all, as the Prince well understands, those skills that are needed to make a good suit are handed down from masters to apprentices in a timeless chain, much like the crown itself.

Below: *The Prince Of Wales receives the editor's Lifetime Achievement Award at the GQ Awards in London, September 2018. The same magazine had previously declared him the world's Best Dressed Man*

Jewel identity

CAROLYN LO

Taiwanese designer Carolyn Lo's handmade, hand-crafted jewellery are timeless pieces that draw from fine art and architecture

"My jewellery speaks for me and connects with people," says Taiwanese jewellery designer Carolyn Lo, who creates one-of-a-kind pieces from her studio in Taipei. "When my customers wear an item of my jewellery, it not only makes them feel beautiful, but it also makes them attract attention. People ask them who has designed it, and that's how my business grows."

A self-taught designer, Carolyn's background was in technology. She studied computer science before working in the airline industry. Travelling gave her a window into other cultures and their art forms, and she discovered a passion for both gemstones and for antiques. In her spare time, she began making jewellery for herself, and her friends and colleagues so admired her designs that they asked her to make jewellery for them too. When the number of orders she was receiving outstripped her ability to fulfil them, Carolyn decided it was time to quit her job and turn her hobby into her career. Six years ago, she opened her studio and become a professional jewellery designer.

All of Carolyn's jewellery is hand-sketched and hand-made, using antique traditions and techniques. "I get a lot of inspiration from painters, especially the Impressionists, like Van Gogh and Monet, and from architecture," she says. "I use all kinds of colours and stones, even diamond slices, without cutting them. For me, stones have to have personality. I don't like standard designs. I like to be different, so whatever else is out there in the market, or that I see other people doing, I deliberately try not to do it!"

Unlike other designers who produce seasonal or themed collections, Carolyn only creates individual pieces, according to her mood and inspiration. "Often, it depends on what stone I'm playing with at that moment. I've just finished a piece I really like, an antique-style cross pendant made using a hundred-year-old European-cut diamond, which I combined with a diamond slice and a rose-cut diamond. It's a combination of old and new." Her latest creation, still a work-in-progress, is a piece inspired by Van Gogh's famous "Starry Night" painting, using a deep blue colour-change garnet, peppered with tiny diamonds and sapphires.

When she takes on commissions for clients, she first likes to get to know the person, their favourite jewellery, taste in clothes, and their personality type. "Sometimes I get a feeling that they'll look better in a bright colour, or a quiet colour. Or I'll encourage them to try something different. Often, they'll say, 'Oh, I didn't realise before that I could – for example – wear long earrings'."

Carolyn classifies her designs as "affordable luxury", with her pieces ranging in price from a few thousand dollars up to $30,000, with most items costing around $10,000. Her jewellery is available to purchase from her website, via her Facebook page and from her studio. In the future she plans to open another studio in London and she is hoping to launch a collection of limited edition pieces – each with its own quirk – for the UK market.

"I see my work more as art than jewellery," she says. "A lot of modern jewellery looks the same. But mine is unique, full of tiny surprising details; I like complicated pieces, not simple ones. Just as the Crown Jewels have lasted centuries and are still cherished today, I hope my jewellery will still be appreciated many years from now."
www.carolynlo.com

Opposite: *Unlike other designers who produce themed collections, Carolyn only creates individual pieces, according to her mood and inspiration*

A pair of Chilstone's Nuneham urns in a country garden, each beautifully weathered like all Chilstone's heritage products

Heavyweight champions

CHILSTONE

Kent-based Chilstone handcrafts fine cast stone for heritage sites and private restorations, including Kensington Palace

When Prince Harry and Meghan Markle announced their engagement in Kensington Palace's Sunken Garden earlier this year, gardening enthusiasts might have admired the four elegant stone planters that framed the royal couple. It was a special moment for the craftsmen at Chilstone who had lovingly created them five years earlier.

"Kensington Palace was refurbished in 2012, and they had some original planters made of pulhamite – a Victorian version of cast stone – which had started crumbling," says Chilstone estimator Andrew Sands. "The Palace wanted 22 planters made, but they wanted them to be scaled down rather than replaced like-for-like, so the new ones would be smaller versions of the originals. We were astonished when Meghan and Harry stood between them to announce their engagement!"

Founded in 1953, Chilstone specialises in creating beautiful garden ornaments. "People usually request our expertise on historical and heritage projects," says Sands. "We've been asked to restore or replace damaged garden pieces and stonework for properties for many clients over the years, bringing back period features to their former glory. Everything's handmade just as it was when we started our business, so we can produce the fine detailing that our clients want."

There are two sides to Chilstone's cast-stone business. One handcrafts garden ornaments, including fountains, planters, pedestals and urns. The other specialises in architectural stonework, including door and window surrounds, string course and gate piers. As well as Kensington Gardens, Chilstone's workmanship can be seen at numerous prestigious venues, including Hever Castle, Sir Roy Strong's Laskett Gardens and the Magna Carta memorial at Runnymede. They've even supplied stonework for various film and TV sets,

from *EastEnders* to Disney's forthcoming *Artemis Fowl* film to the third series of the Netflix drama *The Crown*.

Other major projects over the years have included replacing the urns that adorn the roof of the Temperate House in Kew Gardens after many had been damaged in storage, forgotten in the decades after they were taken down during The Blitz. These are still in place today. Florence's Nightingale's old estate, Embley Park, had a dilapidated urn that featured in a photograph with Florence herself, and wanted it to be replicated to its original splendor. Chilstone used the old urn to painstakingly transfer the original detailed pattern onto the new piece by hand.

"The great thing about working here is that no two days are the same," says General Manager Steve Clark. "We work on a variety of projects, from designing new garden ornaments to restoring period details and making modern features for new-build homes. We value all our customers."

Many of Chilstone's clients have smaller budgets. "Because we're such a compact team of just under two dozen staff, we have the flexibility to mix and match our product range or create something more cost effective to achieve the design our clients want," says Clark. "We can usually do most things, and the team is very innovative about finding creative solutions."

Chilstone is gaining a reputation for creativity. In-house engraver Nigel Hartfield has transformed a stone bench with the iconic *Charlie & Lola* characters for the bestselling author Lauren Child, while sculptor Admir Sljivic's marble resin statue of Leda and The Swan was shortlisted for Product of the Year at the 2017 RHS Chelsea Flower Show.

Chilstone prides itself on the fact that its pieces are long lasting and weather well. Much like the company itself. *www.chilstone.com*

Metal guru

CURTEIS

Using cutting-edge technology, Curteis provides precious metals for the jewellery sector as well as creating its own luxury pieces

Right: *Henry Curteis,
founder of Curteis*

Left: *As well as providing high-
quality precious metals for the
jewellery industry, Curteis also
creates its own high-end pieces
using computer-aided technology
and 3D printers*

"In July 1975 I left Merton College, Oxford, to join an old school friend near Bristol where we were planning to set up a pottery manufacturing business together," remembers Henry Curteis, eponymous founder of precious metal manufacturer Curteis. "By September I had given up the pottery idea and was selling rings and chains to jewellers instead. My father Roger had sold his dairy herd the year before and was looking for a new venture as well – so he bought a chain-making machine hoping to supply my customers."

So the business was forged – link by link and yard by yard – until it earned its hallmark reputation as the leading chain manufacturer in the country. "Our business was quite small at first, although we soon diversified into other products that jewellers and their customers required," he explains. "Surviving as a manufacturer in this market has required flexibility and willingness to change. Today we supply gold and silverware to everyone from independent retailers and high-street jewellers, to award-winning designers, manufacturers and wholesalers."

Innovative and enterprising though father and son have been, some things never change: the quality and craftsmanship of Curteis precious metals is made to last. "Many of our clients have been with us since the beginning," says Curteis. "In our shared vision for the business, the emphasis was always on quality – and to this day we pride ourselves in supplying a product which is made to a high standard for retailers to sell to their customers with confidence. It may be over 40 years since we first established Curteis but, from that point of view, nothing has changed. There are few brands that manufacture anymore but we are a company which stands proud on its traditional values and believe that providing a quality service is paramount."

In an ever-changing market, Curteis has deftly evolved its technological capabilities to meet the expectations of the modern age. It uses laser welding equipment with computer-aided vision to target the welds, and fine detailed work can be carried out much faster and more accurately than before. It has also invested in a 3D printing system which it uses for small production runs and to produce models for new collections.

"It allows us to work quickly and efficiently with client's projects, and makes it simpler for us to make alterations to designs," Curteis explains. "Investing in these cutting-edge technologies has expanded our capabilities, enabling us to do bespoke work and offer brands and designers a comprehensive manufacturing service. We have had great success with this side of the business, as once-small clients have grown into big businesses once they sub-contract their design and production to us. In turn, they can focus on running their businesses and building their market share, without being fixed at the workbench. It is wonderful to witness and be part of their success in this way."

Moving forward, Curteis's plan is to keep adapting and evolving the business so that it remains continually ahead of the curve. "Our plans are for the business to work long-term – which can only be achieved by keeping ahead of the trends, and finding new markets, products and services for our clients. It is a never-ending challenge, but one which everyone at Curteis is primed and ready to take on." *www.curteis.com*

Carried with style

IVANA BAGS

Ivana Bags counts royalty among its clientele, thanks in no small measure to its uniquely interchangeable "Switchy" panels

Opposite: *Individuality is at the heart of Ivana Bags' elegantly adaptable bags and accessories*

"My bag is more than a beautiful must-have – it is a bag with a mission," says Ivana de Haan, founder and designer of Ivana Bags. That mission is self-expression and the dynamic entrepreneur has put it at the heart of her handbag collection, offering her customers the chance to personalise their bag with interchangeable front panels in a vast array of colours and finishes.

De Haan entered luxury fashion with the aim of creating a new accessories line that chimed with her personal taste. "I love handbags, so I chose to create my own collection to suit my own style," she says. "Also, I was asking myself what makes us happy and a better version of ourselves? That is how I finally arrived at the idea of my bag collection."

When she launched Ivana Bags in 2016, it was with a classic bag in two sizes – Mini Me and the larger Max Me. "My feeling was, why change the model if the design is timeless?" she says. The bags, handmade in Istanbul, combine with a range of "Switchy" panels, which might be made of leather, fabric or suede. "A classic camel leather by day becomes altogether more glamorous by night with a snake-skin or a sequinned Switchy panel," says de Haan. "By changing the Switchy the customer has endless possibilities. They can choose any colour or material they want." De Haan also offers a fully bespoke service for one-off pieces, at which level anything is possible, from diamonds to white gold embellishments.

In 2017, de Haan was asked to create a bespoke handbag for Princess Charlene of Monaco. "I decided that I also wanted to be able to give Prince Albert a present, which is how I came to

design him a tie to match the bag," she says. "I had the chance to present it to the Prince at the Top Marques luxury event that is held each year in Monaco." Men's ties have now become part of de Haan's collection.

De Haan came to the Netherlands as a young child from Serbia. During her early career she launched three successful companies in diverse areas of industry and recruitment. When it came to the next challenge, she was ready for a change of direction. "I wanted to do something completely different with my life," she says, "something from the heart that was creative and done with passion."

Alongside promoting Ivana Bags at leading fashion shows and luxury events across Europe, de Haan also puts her business acumen and drive to good use as a business development mentor and life coach. "I have been invited to speak at events in London, Dubai, Ghana and Amsterdam," she says. "I hope to be able to coach and inspire a lot of people to do what is most achievable with their lives." De Haan has been featured in numerous Dutch magazines and has organised her own business event called Women's Platform by Ivana.

With commissions from royalty, de Haan has her sights set on turning Ivana Bags into a global brand: "an Ivana bag for her and an Ivana tie for him". Her model of an independent, stylish customer who likes to make a statement with their accessories is clearly finding a ready audience. "I hope to inspire all women in the world to live their lives to their full potential. My motto? Dare to be yourself!"

www.ivanabags.com

Stone love

KOHINOOR JEWELLERS

Like its country of origin, India's Kohinoor Jewellers blends influences old and new to distinctive and beautiful effect

Agra is a city steeped in history, famous for the iconic white marble Taj Mahal, built by Mughal emperor Shah Jahan. The former Mughal capital has for centuries also been home to jewellers, artisans and artists inspired by the rich heritage around them.

Family-owned and now in its fifth generation, the exclusive, appointment-only Kohinoor Jewellers creates distinctive pieces for a discerning global clientele. "Our business developed out of our heritage," says owner Ghanshyam Mathur. "Now we work with a contemporary fusion of art and jewellery based on Indian art, architecture and paintings."

The Mathur family's ancestors came to the old walled city of Agra in 1857 with the court of the last Mughal emperor Bahadur Shah Zafar. Since then, the family has collected fine gemstones, jewellery and art, becoming experts in the intricacies of Indian art over the generations. Ghanshyam, like his father before him, is a connoisseur of Indian art collected from diverse regions, periods and religions.

"We never run out of inspiration," he says. "There is so much variety in our past. And, of course, we have the Taj Mahal itself, which was the inspiration for the Taj Signature Collection." Not that all inspiration comes from distant history. "My son Milind and I play golf, so we created a very successful golf-themed collection," he says. "We also created a collection based on Bharatanatyam, a classical Indian dance, using the shapes and elegance of the dancers."

The artistry and love of colour and pattern in Kohinoor's jewellery is expressed through gemstones of the highest quality. "Our jewellery is all about the stones – sapphires from Sri Lanka, for example, and rubies from Burma," says Ghanshyam. "We tend to buy stones in rough form and cut them to our specification." Often Kohinoor's jewellery begins not with a design but with the gemstones themselves, the design serving to enhance and display their particular qualities.

Fifth-generation Ruchira Mathur is Kohinoor's designer and works alongside her brother Milind Mathur, who is a graduate gemologist, certified by the Gemological Institute of America, and the company's Artistic Director. "They both have a flair for working with gemstones," says Ghanshyam, "It's in their blood." Ruchira and Milind bring a western sensibility to the jewellery collections, attuned to the tastes of the international visitors who come to Agra.

"Our jewellery is exposed to worldwide trends," says Ghanshyam. "Our customers demand the best quality and they know their jewellery. They immediately see that we offer very fine pieces." Each collection from Kohinoor Jewellers is one of a kind.

The company also offers a bespoke jewellery service, which is particularly suited to overseas visitors staying in Agra. The combination of stones and choice of settings are discussed and detailed design options created. The finished pieces are then shipped on completion.

Kohinoor Jewellers exactly defines what Ghanshyam calls "contemporary fusion": the perfect setting of expertly cut gemstones, reflecting the cultural and artistic traditions of India, and a stylish ability to bring these strands together in refined contemporary jewellery. "This fusion of modern, bespoke and heritage comes through in all our work," says Ghanshyam. As in-the-know visitors to Kohinoor Jewellers have discovered, the Taj Mahal isn't the only thing of beauty worth seeing in Agra.

www.kohinoorjewellers.com

Kohinoor's jewellery combines a beautiful "fusion of modern, bespoke and heritage"

Fashion forward

REBECCA KELLETT

Inspired by architecture, politics and religion, Rebecca Kellett's adventurous designs are aimed at women of all ages

Opposite: "Fashion can be risky," says Rebecca Kellett, "it can start conversations"

"I want to empower women to feel more confident and not to feel that they have to follow or wear a certain trend," says up-and-coming British fashion designer Rebecca Kellett. Kellett, who grew up in Yorkshire, founded her London-based, eponymous label in 2015, after completing her degree in fashion textiles and print at the University for the Creative Arts Rochester.

Her womenswear is both functional and avant-garde, experimenting with new techniques and structural silhouettes, and working with unconventional fabrics such as spacer mesh, PVC and rubber knits. Her designs are inspired by architecture and technology, and they reflect and combine different cultures, cities and landscapes. For her, both colour and digital print are essential elements.

Kellett's creations have already featured on several international platforms including both British and Italian *Vogue* and the influential websites Show Studio and Not Just a Label, and she has collaborated with designers including Anna-Karin Karlsson, Dr Martens and milliner Piers Atkinson. Her designs have also featured in fashion films, including Quentin Hubert's *Silver Goddesses,* which was nominated for Best Costume Design at the International Fashion Film Awards 2016. "The film was about celebrating age," says Kellett. "It showed that, no matter how old you are, there are no boundaries to what you can wear or to expressing yourself. My customers are women from 15 to their 70s."

In November 2017, Kellett became part of the "Best of British" designers showcase at the Houses of Parliament. "It was an incredible event," she recalls. "I like to document political aspects within my work, such as Brexit. The Houses of Parliament are so full of history, and the contrast with the futuristic modern garments on display was striking."

Although she didn't set out to design "modest" clothes, her work was chosen for an exhibition at the Saatchi Gallery in 2017, portraying how modest fashion can also be fashion forward, even futuristic. Her clothes are currently on display in San Francisco as part of Contemporary Muslim Fashions, the first major museum exhibition to explore the complex, diverse nature of Muslim dress codes. As a result of this interest, she has based herself in the UAE for six months, where she is working for a couture brand and gaining knowledge of the market, as well as having discussions with potential investors.

Rebecca Kellett designs, which range in price between £40 to £1,500, can be purchased from Haute Elan, RebeccaKellett and Luxury Closet. She is planning to show at London Fashion Week and hopes that her collections will soon be available in international department stores. She is also working on a luxury sportswear collection for an American brand.

Kellett's next own-brand collection, which will be launched in early 2019, takes as its theme "Empowerment of the female form". "It's inspired by the way Muslim women dress and the change for them politically, particularly in Saudi Arabia," she explains. The collection will feature modern abayas, coats and dresses in a colour palette of mustard, forest green, electric yellow, dusty pink, ivory and midnight blue, with laser cutting, drapery and her signature prints.

Kellett is clear that she wants to push boundaries. "I don't just want to be another brand that's stocked in department stores," she insists. "Fashion can be risky, it can be political and it can start conversations. I want to make people think, to wonder why I've used a particular fabric, shape or detail, and what historical or cultural element has inspired the piece."
www.rebeccakellett.com

CHAPTER FIFTEEN

Sustainable food

Connecting with the food chain

It is becoming increasingly important that our food and drink is ecologically sustainable, locally sourced and environmentally friendly

From plough to plate

NOURISHING A HEALTHY ATTITUDE

Promoting the knowledge, skills and traditions
that support a sustainable food culture lies at the
heart of the Prince's environmental vision

"You may know that old Welsh proverb, 'Cadw dy ardd – ceidw dy ardd dithau'," said the Prince of Wales in a 2012 speech at the National Botanic Garden of Wales. "It translates as: 'Keep your garden – your garden will keep you'."

Sustainable food and farming have been one of the Prince's preoccupying concerns for more than 30 years. He has been actively involved in several organisations in this field, including the Soil Association, the Federation of City Farms and Community Gardens, The Foundation for Common Land, The Global Crop Diversity Trust, The Gloucestershire Root, Fruit and Grain Society, Garden Organic, the Academy of Culinary Arts, Jamie's Farm and the Specialist Cheesemakers Association, as well as his own Duchy Originals, and has been a prominent champion of organic farming and the "slow food" movement.

"The way we produce that food has to be as sustainable as possible," he told his audience in 2012. "If, like me, you have your sights set firmly on the future, then in the very challenging circumstances of the 21st century we have to see sustainability as much more than just an environmental or 'green' issue. It is an absolutely vital economic issue, one that underpins any attempt to create long-term resilience in a country's food security, particularly as we are now exposing ourselves to increasingly severe climate and weather shocks by failing to act globally on climate change. So genuine sustainability is central to safeguarding jobs and promoting the rural economy. But it must do this in an integrated way."

The Prince has raised concerns about modern culture's disconnection from the world of agriculture. "Over the last 40 years it would appear that we have managed to create a whole generation whose understanding of where food comes from and how it is produced is severely limited," he said to a Soil Association function in 2008. "And it is causing real harm. The over-reliance on packaged, processed food is not just damaging our own health, but damaging our bio-diversity, our soil through agro-chemicals and our water-table through pesticides. And, linked to all this, our family farmers have seen ever-diminishing returns on their produce, which means that rural communities have suffered from the loss of local distinctiveness, traditions and culture."

Speaking at BBC Radio 4's Food And Farming Awards in 2009, he acknowledged the battle faced by champions of organic and sustainable farming. "I do understand why the lure of industrially produced food is so attractive to some people, all of whom I am convinced have the best of intentions," he said. "But I think it is very important that society recognises the true cost, not just in environmental terms, but also in terms of its impact on our own health. If we lose the essential balance and disrupt the virtuous circle, then we risk incurring long-term and unmanageable costs."

He went on to celebrate smaller scale, local and sustainable food production, drawing a distinction between what he calls "agri-culture" and "agri-industry". "If we lose the knowledge, skills and traditions of our food culture, and we fail to give back to the soil and to Nature what we take from them, we will lose the wherewithal to look after ourselves and our planet," said the Prince. "How we grow food and then distribute it can make the whole difference to carbon emissions and it is the responsibility of each and every link in the food chain, from plough to plate to find ways to reduce its impact on the environment."

Below: *The Prince of Wales talks with local children at the Common Good City Farm in Washington, DC in May 2011. The urban farm provides food and education for low-income neighbourhood residents*

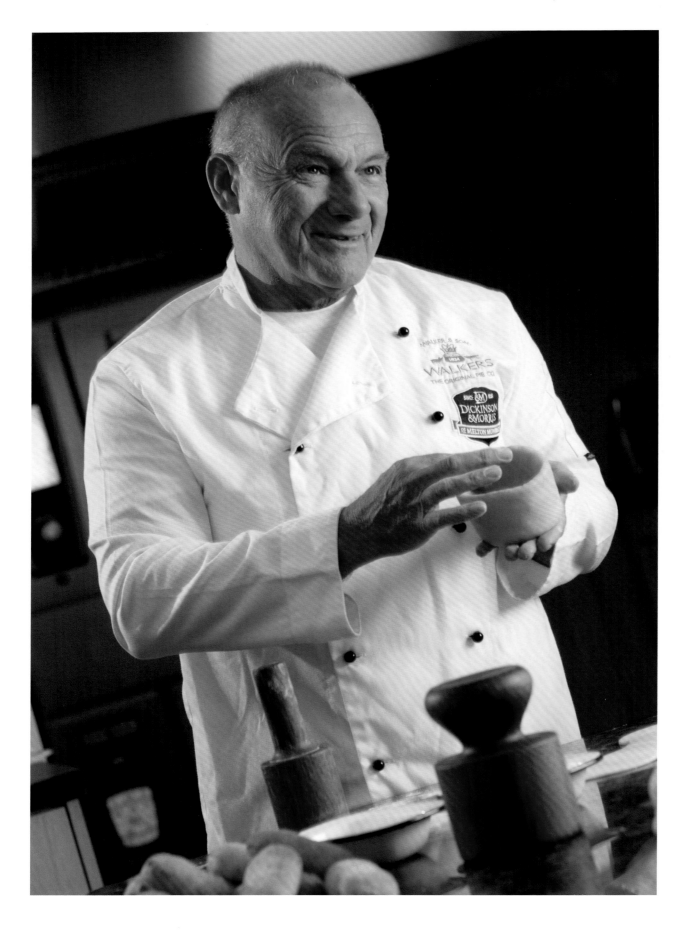

Local hero

SAMWORTH BROTHERS

Samworth Brothers, one of Britain's biggest chilled-food manufacturers, is committed to its local communities and assorted UK charities

Opposite: Samworth Brothers has been forging responsible links with the British food and farming community for more than a century

For more than a century, Samworth Brothers has had three values that underpin its activities: a commitment to local communities, a strong sense of ambition and a determination to innovate. These principles inform not only the company's business affairs, manufacturing much-loved brands like Ginsters and Soreen and quality food for leading retailers, but also its commitment to sustainability and the environment.

This springs from the company's origins deep within the UK food and farming community. Samworth Brothers was founded in the 1890s by George Samworth and through four generations the family-owned business has supported UK food and farming while demonstrating strong entrepreneurial flair.

This belief in community and sustainability has seen Samworth Brothers work alongside both the Prince's Trust and the Prince's Countryside Fund. Samworth Brothers has a strong presence in Cornwall and as a result has been involved with a variety of Prince's Trust programmes designed to help young people get into jobs, education and training. The work with the Countryside Fund has been equally important.

"A lot of our raw materials come out the ground and we have a very close relationship with many farming communities," says Group Executive Board Director Mary-Ann Kilby. "We have worked with the Prince's Countryside Fund and Business in the Community, and have been a lead sponsor of the Rural Action Award. It reflects our own approach. We like to ensure that, right through our supply chain, we are looking after homegrown produce and people."

The company approaches environmental issues with the same forward-thinking, creative, positive attitude that it applies to the more commercial aspects of the business. Samworth Brothers' environmental communication and action programme is known simply as The 4R Plan. This focuses on delivering continual improvements through reducing impact, reusing resources, recycling materials and adopting recovery principles. Ambitious targets have been set, such as halving food waste from production by 2030 and achieving 90 per cent total reuse/recycling across the group by the end of 2020. Some targets have already been met, such as obtaining 100 per cent of purchased electricity sourced from natural renewable sources.

Samworth Brothers believes in sustainability because it believes in people. This is demonstrated by the company's charitable enterprises. One flagship programme is the biennial Charity Challenge, a sponsored triathlon that has so far raised £1.9 million for charitable enterprises since it was launched. There's also the Sports Opportunity Fund, which was launched in November 2013. The fund helps sponsor sports clubs with the view that young people can develop confidence, self-esteem and better life skills through sport. It has so far delivered more than 130 awards totalling more than £1.7 million to over 75 organisations in locations where there is a strong Samworth Brothers presence, most particularly in Leicester, Cornwall and Greater Manchester. Samworth Brothers also works with local schools, mentoring secondary school and college pupils on interview techniques and CV writing while working to close the skills gaps in STEM (science, technology, engineering, maths) subjects through STEM ambassadors.

Then there is the food. Samworth Brothers is always looking at innovative ways it can develop its offering to its retailer customers and consumers, both in terms of value and taste, with its wide range of high-quality food products. It is also proud to be a great supporter of British food heritage (including traditional British favourites such as the Melton Mowbray pork pie and the Cornish pasty) and the wider British food and farming community.
www.samworthbrothers.co.uk

Crème de la crème

A.E. RODDA & SON LIMITED

With the Royal Family among its many fans,
A.E. Rodda & Son has been crafting its sumptuous
Cornish clotted cream for five generations

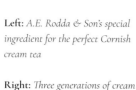

Left: *A.E. Rodda & Son's special ingredient for the perfect Cornish cream tea*

Right: *Three generations of cream makers – the Rodda family*

When Nicholas Rodda considers the best way to prepare a traditional Cornish cream tea, he selects his words carefully. "You break the warm scone in half, place on the jam, then carefully spoon the clotted cream on top," he says. "It's a cream tea, so the cream should be the crowning feature." Rodda should know. As the Managing Director of Rodda's he is the fifth generation of his family to run a company that has been producing Cornish clotted cream on its original site in Scorrier, Cornwall for more than a century. What began as a kitchen enterprise of Nicholas's great great-grandmother Eliza Jane Rodda has now become a hugely successful business that produces in the region of 250 million spoonfuls of clotted cream a year, supplying not just hotels and restaurants in the UK but venues as far afield as Japan, Hong Kong, Dubai and Australia.

A Cornish cream tea remains a special occasion, often enjoyed when holidaying in Cornwall. It's one reason why customers look on Rodda's so fondly – it represents a moment when a family comes together to enjoy something memorable. Those fans include members of the Royal Family. Rodda's clotted cream was served at the Royal Wedding in 1981 and Prince Charles requested eight ounces of Rodda's Cornish clotted cream was sent to the Queen Mother every week for over 20 years. "We are very proud of our royal connections particularly as Prince Charles is the Duke of Cornwall," says Rodda. "We are delighted that Cornish clotted cream has helped to put Cornish food on the world stage."

The Duke of Edinburgh still sends Rodda's cream to a select number of close friends every Christmas, and the company has supplied other royal weddings and events. However, when the Palace contacted Rodda's in the early '90s to request some butter, the company found it had a problem. "We didn't actually make butter at that time," says Rodda. "But the Queen was very keen so we felt obliged and went into butter making. We now sell butter to various outlets including farm shops and delis. We might not have done that without the Queen's request, so we feel privileged to have Her Majesty as part of our product-development team!"

The company has a strong commitment to sustainability, a subject close to the Prince's heart. "We've always believed it makes sense to save natural resources so good environmental practice is embedded into our ethos," says Rodda. "Compared to many other working creameries, we know that we only use about a fraction of the water and we are working to reduce this still further. We continually strive to be as sustainable as possible and work closely with our farming families to share sustainability best practice with the aim of protecting the environment for future generations."

Rodda's still operates adjacent to Eliza Jane Rodda's original farmhouse, and all its milk is supplied by local farms within a 30 mile radius of the creamery. "We work with local farmers to ensure farming has a secure future and the quality of our clotted cream depends upon the richness of the milk from the lush green pastures of Cornwall," says Rodda. "The Rodda family has passed on the same values down through the generations: each has made some changes but none of us will lose sight of our heritage. After all, our name is on every pot that leaves the creamery."
www.roddas.co.uk

Source of pride

HILDON

A passion for the wider environment lies at the heart of Hildon's award-winning bottled waters

The story of Hildon natural mineral water, served in some of the best restaurants and hotels around the world, is one that starts and ends in the idyllic Test Valley in Hampshire. Just as terroir is essential to the character of a great wine, the terroir on the 160-acre Hildon Estate gives this natural mineral water its award-winning clean, clear taste. As much care goes into sustaining the soil quality, the trees and the wildlife on the estate as it does in maintaining the integrity of its precious water.

Bottled at source means exactly what it says. Hildon water is brought up from a 75-metre deep aquifer and is bottled on site. "We are not allowed to change the water's composition," says Executive Director Debbie Jones. "It travels through underground pipes and does not see the light of day until it meets the bottle. You would hardly even know the wellhead was there."

It takes some 50 years of natural filtration through chalk hills to achieve Hildon's palette-cleansing clarity. It is low in sodium and maintains a unique balance of nutrients and minerals. Hildon was one of the first companies to requalify for the latest environmental and quality assessments outlined by the ISO (International Organisation for Standardisation).

When the late owner Christian Heppe bought Hildon House, the presence of an aquifer on the land was an unexpected bonus. His idea for an upmarket bottled water resulted in the first turquoise-labelled, Bordeaux-style bottles being produced in 1989. Since then, Delightfully Still and Gently Sparkling have been the only bottled waters to win the *Restaurant* Magazine Award six consecutive times; and, in 2017, Hildon Ltd was proud to be granted a Royal Warrant from Her Majesty The Queen as a Supplier of Natural Mineral Water.

Hildon is also a proud supporter of the Roux Scholarship for the next generation of leading chefs. "Christian Heppe was a philanthropic founder," says Jones. "His ethos, morals and integrity are still everywhere in the business. Protecting the natural environment surrounding Hildon's headquarters is about looking after the land and sustaining the wildlife on it for the future. We are like a family here and we would like future generations to enjoy what we have today."

Mindful of the declining bee population, Hildon now has approximately 120,000 bees living in three new colonies. "We worked with Hampshire & Isle of Wight Wildlife Trust to get started," says Jones, who attended a bee-keeping course with her colleagues. "We are still learning together and plan to improve our bee-keeping skills. The bees are happy and we even got some honey last year."

Sustainability is carefully monitored with more than 90 per cent of waste being recycled. "All glass goes back to the furnace, caps are recycled and a removal firm reuses our redundant cardboard boxes," says Jones. "We also use AdBlue for our diesel trucks to reduce emissions."

Following the success of Hildon Ltd, The Hildon Foundation was formed and now contributes to a variety of local charities and good causes including schools, wildlife projects, a children's hospice and a cardiac centre. "It's always been about giving something back," says Jones. "Our owner is equally keen about the land and the people living here, so the drive to continue to support our environment remains high on the agenda." That passion resonates through the energy of the current team of 60 working on the Hildon estate, whether they are producing a world-class product, tending the bees or maintaining their patch of rural beauty for the next generation. *www.hildon.com*

Above: *Sunrise on a beautiful frosty morning on the Hildon Estate*

Right: *Sourced in rural Hampshire, Hildon is a fixture in many of London's top restaurants*

Highland gains

BAXTERS FOOD GROUP

For 150 years, Baxters has brought authentic
Scottish specialities to millions around the world
– including the royal household

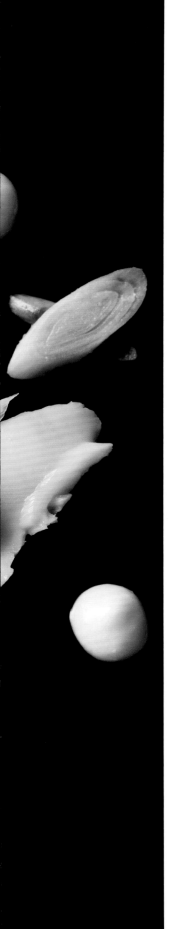

Right: *Baxters uses the smoked haddock of SJ Edwards, based in nearby Lossiemouth, for its Cullen skink soups*

"Purveyors of Scottish Specialities" reads the Royal Warrant granted to Baxters by the Queen in 1955 and proudly held ever since. Among the specialities supplied to the royal household are raspberries grown in Fife and plums from the nearby Gordon Castle Estate. The ongoing commitment to sourcing high-quality produce from Scottish suppliers for its soups, preserves and chutneys is at the heart of Baxters' success as it celebrates its 150th anniversary.

"From our beginnings in 1868 as a small grocery store, Baxters Food Group has grown into a global business, as well as one of the nation's most treasured brands," says Audrey Baxter, Executive Chairman, Group CEO and fourth generation of the family firm. "Our royal warrant is in recognition of our commitment to producing food of the highest quality. We are as proud of this now as we were all those years ago."

When Audrey's great grandfather George and his wife Margaret set up their grocery shop in Fochabers in 1868 with a £100 family loan, their mission to "be different, be better" became the foundation of the business's expansion and product innovation. As long ago as 1923, Baxters was the first Scottish company to can raspberries and strawberries and in 1962 Baxters became the first UK company to introduce twist-top caps on 12oz jars of preserves. Today Baxters continues to invest in developing efficient, lightweight and fully recyclable packaging.

However ingenious the packaging, it is of course what is inside it that customers appreciate. Baxters produces around 150 products and is constantly reviewing and improving its range. Audrey Baxter is involved at every stage of the process, whether refining an old favourite or developing something new. Only when completely satisfied will she put her name to a new recipe. The Audrey Baxter signature range includes specialities such as lobster bisque with brandy and double cream, or passionfruit and mango curd.

Baxters sources ingredients from all over the world, but is particularly proud of the sustainable, long-term relationships is has built up with local suppliers. For more than 50 years it has bought the North Sea smoked haddock for its Cullen skink from SJ Edwards, who smokes the fish a few miles from Fochabers.

"We're proud to be a trusted, local supplier to a company with a history that is so deeply rooted in Scotland," says owner Billie Edwards. Local suppliers for some of its other products include David Brown Farms for beetroot, swedes and carrots from Maxwell Farms, and double cream produced in Nairn, just 20 miles away.

Baxters has carried the ethos of sustainable and ethical sourcing into its support for overseas initiatives such as Good Greens in India and Green Team in the Ukraine, where its understanding of the food supply chain is helping develop ethical production strategies in those communities.

Closer to home, The Gordon and Ena Baxter Foundation supports arts, heritage, environmental and sports projects in northern Scotland. "It has provided education and training, particularly to young entrepreneurs working with The Prince's Trust," says Audrey. "It is a way of giving back to the local communities where we first laid the foundations of our family business."

When Baxters turned 125, the Duke of Rothesay, a kilted Prince Charles, was guest of honour in Fochabers. "Now here we are 25 years later, commemorating our milestone birthdays together," says Audrey. "As we celebrate our 150th anniversary, our mission to 'be different, be better' is more relevant than ever." *www.baxters.com*

Food of the future

McDONALD'S CORPORATION

McDonald's is using its scale and influence to effect positive environmental change throughout its entire supply chain

As the world's largest restaurant company, with 36,000 locations across more than 100 countries, McDonald's is using its influence to tackle today's pressing social and environmental issues. Taking its cue from the United Nations' Sustainable Development Goals (SDGs), the McDonald's Scale for Good programme is addressing sustainability throughout its supply chain, focusing on critical issues that are important for people, anials and the planet, such as waste reduction, recycling and protecting farmers, forests and fisheries.

"We see the SDGs as a roadmap for McDonald's global sustainability strategy," says McDonald's Vice President Sustainability Keith Kenny. He acknowledges that achieving a sustainable supply chain takes time and commitment. "It's about innovation and continuous improvement and partnering with suppliers, producers, restaurant owners and employees."

Of the UN's 17 SDGs, McDonald's recognises climate change as the biggest environmental issue of our time. It is one of five SDGs, including protecting forests and farmer livelihoods, that the company is focusing on. "These are big areas where we decided we could drive transformational change beyond our own business," says Kenny. Current President and CEO Steve Easterbrook, formerly head of McDonald's UK, has long been a supporter of environmental initiatives. He was one of the senior business champions of the Prince of Wales's Rainforest Project, a legacy he has brought to the global McDonald's culture.

In the UK, McDonald's has long-term relationships with the farming community and is one of the largest purchasers of raw ingredients; buying, for example, the largest volume of the UK's organic milk for its teas, coffees and Happy Meals. Its close working ties have allowed it to collaborate with farmers on improving food standards and productivity. "All our farmers are Farm Assured,"

says Peter Garbutt, Sustainable Sourcing Manager UK, "and we learn from them just as much as they learn from us."

Since 1998, McDonald's eggs have been free range, but McDonald's and its farmers have gone a step further. "Because hens are jungle birds, they are naturally accustomed to tree cover, so putting them in a field wasn't the most natural environment," says Garbutt. "We invested in peer-reviewed research and found that planting trees has encouraged them to range more, improved their welfare and increased the quality of the yield." To date, this change in policy has resulted in the new planting of half a million trees.

Ninety per cent of McDonald's restaurants are run by franchisees. For Helen McFarlane, Restaurant Sustainability Manager UK, it is a business model based on trust. "We are on a journey to achieve our sustainability goals, and we trust our franchisees to join us on that journey." Like the farmers who supply McDonald's, some franchisees are second- and third-generation families who bring McDonald's values into the communities they serve. From recycling and reducing waste to installing energy-efficient LED lighting, they are part of the collective effort towards sustainability. Transportation is also a vital element of that effort. "All our cooking oil is collected and reprocessed into biodiesel, which fuels our fleet," says McFarlane. "It can be more expensive than normal diesel, but it is the right thing to do."

In March 2018, McDonald's became the first restaurant company globally to set itself a science-based target to significantly reduce greenhouse gas emissions in line with the Paris Climate Agreement. "We're all about valuing and preserving the planet's natural resources, from forestry to agriculture, and ensuring the integrity of our supply chain," says Kenny. "Our policy is always to influence positive change."

corporate.mcdonalds.com/corpmcd.html

McDonald's Progressive Young Farmers programme provides year-long mentorship to undergraduate students

Food for thought

BIDFOOD

Food wholesaler Bidfood is using its influence in the catering industry to initiate progressive, sustainable policies

Left: *Bidfood has won recognition for its sustainable approach to food*

Right: *The company operates a regionally decentralised approach, with 23 sites around the UK*

Bidfood is one of the UK's largest food wholesalers and, as such, influences the quality and provenance of what many food outlets sell. Servicing over 40,000 customers across the UK with more than 13,000 products, Bidfood prides itself on providing the best of own-brand and leading food-service brands, offering customers nutritional information, menu ideas, advice and guidance on food standards and legislation.

Bidfood promotes sustainable business practices that help reduce waste and protect the environment – something that won it recognition at the recent Planet Mark awards. Whether it's by reducing single-use plastics or increasing its range of vegan produce, Bidfood responds quickly and effectively to meet environmental concerns and customer demands.

"Lots of people deliver food," says CEO Andrew Selley. "We constantly aim to deliver service excellence to our customers to make their lives easier and help their businesses grow." One customer is the Royal Household, from whom Bidfood has held a Royal Warrant since 1955. "It's still a privilege," says Selley. "We work closely with the head chef at the palace, who will, at times, have slightly different requirements to the usual customer."

At the heart of Bidfood's operation is the duty to work for its customers. It runs three "customer experience" centres, with open kitchens and barista bars that demonstrate new products, point-of-sale materials and professional equipment. The company website features regularly updated menus tailored to shifts in the nation's eating habits, with 300–400 vegetarian, vegan and gluten-free products.

Bidfood operates 23 sites across the UK. A decentralised approach allows it to work with regional businesses. "Scotland is a good example," says Selley. "Our Scottish depot started working with a local cake and dessert supplier for their local market. It was so successful that we now sell these products around the UK." Food origins and provenance are a high priority, and Bidfood supplies Red Tractor Assured meat for its Farmstead range and fish certified by the Marine Stewardship Council. The company is also committed to helping consumers make healthy choices. It supports aims to reduce sugar consumption and has developed its own sugar-management pledge with the support of Public Health England. It has reduced the sugar content in its own ice cream range by 23 per cent.

Bees pollinate 70 of the core 100 food crops that humans eat and Bidfood's "To Bee or Not to Bee" campaign raises awareness of how serious an issue the declining bee population is. The company received a Corporate Social Responsibility Award at the Foodservice Packaging Association awards for its work supporting bee keepers, installing hives and bee hotels at some of its depots, and donating sugar to feed bees.

Bidfood continually evolves its sustainability programme, Food for the Future, which aligns to the UN's Sustainable Development Goals. The company ensures that its own-brand Springbourne water comes in bottles containing 50 per cent recycled plastic. It also signed up to the Courtauld Commitment in 2016, which aims to reduce food and drink waste by 20 per cent by 2025.

Since 2013, Bidfood has been the driving force behind the plate2planet website, which encourages its business partners to share advice and experience about their environmental initiatives and strategies to reduce waste. "Action on sustainability can't be pushed down from the top," says Selley. "We engage 90 members of our staff as Sustainability Coordinators. We've already achieved a 13.7 per cent reduction in our carbon footprint since 2017." Producing food that is delicious, healthy and sustainable is the ambition that drives Bidfood. Winning Wholesaler of the Year at Grocer Gold Awards in 2018 and The Grocer Cup at the Institute of Grocery Distribution awards suggests that the company's business model is fit for the future.
www.bidfood.co.uk

Baking history

WALKERS SHORTBREAD

Walkers Shortbread has established itself as the world's favourite Scottish shortbread, with members of the Royal Family among its fans

Left: *Walkers Shortbread uses just four ingredients: flour, butter, sugar and salt*

"The name doesn't explain it too well," says Jim Walker, Joint Managing Director of Walkers Shortbread. "A shortbread is neither a biscuit nor a cake nor a bread. It should be crunchy and sweet, but not too sweet. It should be substantial yet melt-in-the-mouth. In short, it should have character as it is indigenous to Scotland."

Made with four simple ingredients – flour, butter, sugar and salt – this unique Scottish confection has been baked by the Walker family since 1898, when Jim's grandfather Joseph Walker first established the business.

"He borrowed £50, which, at the time, was just enough money to take rent of a small shop in Deeside, and buy some raw materials and equipment," explains Jim. "He always was a gifted baker, and his ambition was to make the finest shortbread in the world."

Operations moved from Deeside to Speyside in 1910 and the next generation soon took over. Yet by the time Jim and his two siblings, Joseph and Marjorie, joined the business in the early 1960s, it was still a humble village bakery producing delicious local shortbread.

"We only employed 16 people at that time and we lived above the shop," says Jim. "But we worked well together as a team, with Joe taking care of production, Marjorie looking after finance, and myself on sales."

The business grew through word-of-mouth and sales increased steadily, as visitors to the area began buying Walkers Shortbread and taking it back to London with them. Now the fifth generation of Walkers have begun learning the ropes in this major family business, which operates six factories in Speyside and employs almost 1,700 people during peak times.

In essence, nothing has changed. Permanently rooted to their scenic location in the beautiful Scottish highlands, the Walkers' family vision is still to make the finest shortbread in the world and to remain an independent family business within their local community.

"It's about doing a simple thing well with honesty and integrity," says Jim. "Our absolute focus is on the quality of our product, and we try to attract sustainable business so that we can foster long-term growth and employment."

Walkers now produces a number of popular shortbread varieties, including shortbread rounds with an iconic Scottish thistle stamped on each highlander shortbread rolled in demerara sugar, and their famous shortbread fingers, which are recognised the world over.

"We began to export our products in 1975 and found that it took us 40 years to become an overnight success," says Jim. "As a result, we are the only ambient UK food manufacturer to have won the Queen's Award for Export Achievement on four occasions."

It's not the only royal recognition it has had to date. In addition to receiving multiple royal visitors over the years – including Prince Charles opening three of its factories – Walkers was invited to partner with Prince Charles in 1990 to create his signature Duchy Originals organic biscuits.

In 2002 Walkers was granted a Royal Warrant from Her Majesty the Queen for the supply of oatcakes. Yet the real prizewinner at Walkers remains the company's shortbread, which received a Royal Warrant from the Queen in 2017. "We were the first company to specialise in shortbread: perhaps because it represents only 5 per cent of the biscuit market," says Jim. "It may be niche, but we put traditional Scottish shortbread on the map. And of that, we're extremely proud."
www.walkersshortbread.com

CHAPTER SIXTEEN

Global hospitality
Entertaining in style

Be it luxury resorts, high-end hotels or the quality food and drinks designed for elite parties, hospitality is helping to bring the world together

Abroad appeal

THE GLOBAL AMBASSADOR

The Prince's developing role as Her Majesty's representative, at home and abroad, has seen him take on an increasing number of royal duties in recent years

Over the last 70 years, Prince Charles has become one of the most travelled men on earth, clocking up thousands of miles on royal visits since his childhood. Since his investiture as the Prince of Wales in 1969 these have often been official visits, or public engagements in service of charities: either the 14 charitable organisations of which he is president, or the 400 or more charities of which he is a patron.

As Her Majesty The Queen winds down her gruelling schedule of public engagements – reducing her official events from 332 in 2016 to 296 in 2017 – Prince Charles's travel has increased as he starts to represent the sovereign on many official visits. With the Duke of Edinburgh now officially retired from royal engagements and the Queen rarely, if ever, travelling abroad, Prince Charles's engagements have increased. In 2015, the Prince attended 99 seminars, luncheons and dinners in the name of duty, visiting more than 75 towns and cities around the UK. In 2017, the 69-year-old Prince clocked up 619 engagements in the UK and 15 other countries. He regularly travels more than 60,000 miles on official business each year.

He has certainly benefited from the hospitality of others: in 2013 alone, his documented gifts included a silk tie, a portable water filtration kit and a bag of dried organic apple rings. He has also become an expert in offering hospitality to others – in 2015 he and Camilla, Duchess of Cornwall, hosted more than 6,000 guests at events at their numerous royal residences.

There have been many fanciful stories about the Prince's travel requirements. Tom Bower's biography, *Rebel Prince*, suggests that Charles travels with a retinue that includes a butler, a chef, two valets, a private secretary, a typist and several bodyguards. There are also stories about him arriving at friends' houses accompanied by a truck carrying suitcases, an orthopaedic bed, bedlinen, furniture, a radio, Kleenex Velvet toilet roll, Laphroaig whisky, a toilet seat and even landscapes of the Scottish countryside.

Charles has laughed off these stories, and aides have denied most of these requirements, although it's certainly true that the Prince enjoys travelling in some style. In autumn 2017, he and Camilla commissioned the Voyager A330 private jet – nicknamed Cam Force One after the former Prime Minister David Cameron, who sanctioned it – for a two-week tour of Singapore, Malaysia, Brunei and India. "The Prince of Wales is also representing Her Majesty, and it is therefore important that the form of transport is appropriate," said a spokesperson from Clarence House. "There are those who might say it is right that visits of this sort should be assisted by the Royal Air Force. I don't think it's about being grand, it's about security, efficiency and value for money and delivering the programme."

As well as serving as an ambassador abroad for the United Kingdom, Prince Charles serves as a champion of tourism for various British causes. As well as serving as President of the National Trust, he serves as a Patron of the North Highland Initiative promoting tourism to Scotland. "While, of course, the tourist industry is keen to attract visitors from abroad," said the Prince, "I can only hope that every effort will be made to remind the people of this country just what wonderful opportunities for holidays they have on their doorsteps, without having to leave our shores."

Opposite: Prince Charles, the Duke of Rothesay, visits Mackintosh At The Willow Tea Rooms in Glasgow, September 2018, promoting the UK as a destination for national and international holidaymakers

The heavenly hostess

LAUREN BERGER COLLECTION

Lauren Berger has a passion for hospitality,
artfully matching her guests around the world
with spectacular accommodation

Left: *A home in the Dominican Republic, West Indies, one of Lauren Berger's many luxury properties*

Right: *Lauren with her husband, Dr Sidney Berger*

In the world of luxury travel, certain things are a given – lavish accommodation, extensive amenities and excellent service. But, for Lauren Berger, the hospitality offered to guests of Lauren Berger Collection goes far beyond this. "Hospitality is really what I'm made of," she says. "This is not just my business, it's my life. If I only had a day to live, I'd spend that day taking care of my guests."

With around 300 select properties in more than 20 locations worldwide, Berger prides herself on finding the perfect home for each guest; homes that are not only elegant and sophisticated but also the perfect fit for the guests staying there. "I was born to take care of people," she says. "It's not just what I do for a living. I take care and decorate for my guests to make them feel like they never left the comfort of their own home."

Lauren Berger Collection is underpinned by the philosophy of personalised hospitality, where a guest's every whim is fulfilled, and the team combines discretion with efficient service. A 20-hour day is not uncommon for New York-based Berger, as she responds to emails and requests from guests from around the world, from Hong Kong to Brazil. However, the most important thing is that individual touch. "I try to spend as much time as I can getting to know my guests before their arrival," she says. "Detailing in my homes is not just about comfortable beds, pillows, and blankets. It's about paying close attention to their needs, whatever they might be."

From the Hamptons to the Caribbean, from Paris to the Adriatic, the international properties offered by Lauren Berger Collection are spectacular. These include the magical vacation home in Westhampton Beach, New York. One of the latest luxurious additions is Chalet des Sens in Megeve in the

French Alps, whose unique quality, copious splendour and unrivalled level of comfort make for an unforgettable stay and a devoted clientele.

"This outstanding chalet is truly one of a kind, with an appearance that's worthy of a piece of art," says Berger. "A ski-in, ski-out chalet, it's one of the most extraordinary and most elegant homes in the world for rent. Its quality, location, and offering of a service so caring and respectful that it makes every guest feel like royalty mean there is no competition. We couldn't be more proud of our collaboration with the Chalet des Sens – a winter haven that's fit for a king."

Lauren Berger Collection offers membership programmes, while regular guests and those enjoying lengthy stays are rewarded with VIP Ambassador Concierge Service and the option to include yachts, luxury vehicles, and classic sports cars. No request is too difficult, be it private-jet services, a 24-hour butler, an in-house chef and sommelier or a crew for a luxury yacht. "There's nothing I love more than taking care of my guests," says Berger. "There are no limitations whatsoever, no boundaries. If it's legal, if it's possible, it's done."

The collection is expected to expand, enabling more guests to experience these outstanding levels of service and hospitality. "Some of the grandest families from around the world would like Lauren Berger Collection to represent their properties," says Berger. "They own outstanding properties that have never been on the market."

Whether these properties belong to royalty or the tech elite, Berger ensures every guest is given a welcome to prove the truth of her motto – "never leave home".

www.laurenbergercollection.com

Spirit of ecstasy

D1 LONDON

D1 London creates beautifully packaged, flavoursome gins, vodkas and cold-infusion pockets for a global market

"My passion is about creating things and seeing concept brought into reality," says Dominic Limbrey, founder and owner of premium spirits company D1 London. The initial concept was sparked several years ago when Dominic was working for another British gin brand and looking at their supply routes into Asia. He had the realisation that many of the products available in the market didn't fit the tastes of the international consumer and wanted to shake things up.

"British gins are traditionally dominated by strong, bold botanicals that can taste quite bitter," Dominic explains. "I wanted to create something more elegant – something softer and smoother, which nonetheless retained the juniper and botanical flavours that are typical of gin. Our gin is a classic London dry citrus base with a two-step flavour profile. The taste is long and mellow with a variety of sweet and spicy botanicals, including nettle – a contemporary addition – which adds a soft, earthy, tannic flavour. People describe it is as wonderfully smooth and refreshing."

Buoyed by the success of D1 London Gin, Dominic decided he wanted to create something new with vodka. Using potato (which has a natural velvety texture) instead of traditional grain for distillation, D1 produced a beautifully smooth and rounded vodka with elements of sweetness and some spice to finish.

"Vodka is less synonymously British than gin," Dominic admits, "but brand Britain has an eclectic identity constructed from its days of being a travelling nation. Likewise, although D1 Potato Vodka is initially distilled elsewhere, the final distillation takes place in the UK and this is where everything is assembled. The bottles may be produced in France, the caps made in Italy, and the printing done in Scotland, but the final product is proudly British."

Dominic, whose background is in design and engineering, collaborated with international pop artist Jacky Tsai to design the trademark D1 bottles and packaging in a flourish of inspiration.

"The art Jacky produces is unique," he enthuses. "He loves to play with ideas of contrast and juxtaposition – so, the signature blue floral skull on our gin bottle represents death and decay but also the beauty of life and growth. Likewise, the brightly coloured stained glass skull on our vodka bottle alludes to Mexican Day Of The Dead festivities, but it is also deeply rooted in the Christian tradition."

From product to branding, innovation fuels the creativity behind D1 London. Taken with a consumer appetite for more interesting and complex flavours, Dominic recently launched D1's Cold Infusions in six different hand-blended flavour profiles. "I'd been watching what was going on in the mixer market and felt concerned by the large amounts of sugar used – it supresses the fundamental flavours of things and ruins their integrity," he says. "Using the idea of the teabag as our model, we invented cold-infusion pockets which can be added to spirits or soda water to produce wonderfully high-integrity flavour with no artificial colours or flavours."

Flavour combinations include zingy citrus balanced with the sweetness of orange and lime, passionfruit with vanilla and orange, seasonal summer fruits, and five spices with an earthy rooibos base. "Our gin and vodka are very palatable and don't require the same level of sweetness to be added to them, so these cold infusion pockets make the perfect pairing," he adds. "They're also ideal for mixing non-alcoholic cocktails for a more grown-up drinking experience."

d1londonspirits.co.uk

Be it gin or vodka, D1 London brings a very British passion to the spirit sector

Archaeological Paths provides its guests with access to historical sites that are often closed to the general public

Travel like royalty

ARCHAEOLOGICAL PATHS

Guided by some of the world's most renowned experts, Archaeological Paths' unique tours offer exclusive insights into the ancient world

"The culture and thinking that flourished in Ancient Egypt 5,000 years ago could be called a foundation culture," wrote Prince Charles in his 2010 book, *Harmony*. "It is a source of our mythology and religious symbolism, our astronomy, geometry and mathematics, even the shape of our letters. They are all distant echoes of an outlook that defined a people whose life revolved completely around the ebb and flow of the mighty Nile."

The Prince of Wales is just one of many to be intrigued by this ancient civilisation. "Egypt's treasures and cultural heritage have been fascinating people for centuries," says the renowned archaeologist Dr Zahi Hawass. "And no one can tour Egypt quite like Archaeological Paths. With us, you will visit many unique sites that very few people can see. You will be treated like royalty; this is why we call it the Royal Tour."

Dr Hawass, one of *Time* magazine's Top 100 Most Influential People In The World, is just one of the prestigious experts behind Archaeological Paths, a company that offers exclusive, in-depth tours of Egypt. The company's offerings include the luxury 14-day Royal Tour, which takes a small group of guests to places that are normally closed to visitors. It also organises tours for VIPs and Hollywood stars.

"Enthusiasts visit the Land of the Pharaohs to see places hidden from the public eye and gain access to places that are closed to the public," says Dr Hawass. "Who wouldn't like to stand between the paws of the Great Sphinx? Who wouldn't like to visit subterranean chamber in the Great Pyramid that nobody else will get to see? I believe there is no better way to visit Egypt than the Royal Tour."

Archaeological Paths was founded in 2003 by travel professionals who wanted to share their passion for archaeology and history. What distinguishes its Royal Tour from other offerings is a commitment to getting under the skin of the country without ever stinting on quality. That can mean exploring temples at Karnak and Abu Simbel with archaeological experts in cooperation with the Ministry of Antiquities. It can also mean staying in a five-star hotel in the shadow of the pyramids, sailing up the Nile on luxury cruise ships and experiencing the finest cuisine Egypt has to offer.

The tours start and end in Cairo and take in all the major Egyptian sites, from the Great Pyramids of Giza to the extraordinary sites in the southern city of Aswan along the River Nile. The trip includes visits to UNESCO World Heritage sites at Luxor and the Valley of the Kings, as well as museums and temples. One of the experts is Dr Mostafa Waziri, the man currently responsible for all the antiquities and archaeological sites in Egypt. There is even a chance to meet Jehan Sadat, wife of Egypt's late president Anwar El-Sadat, in the former presidential residence. This gives visitors further insight into Egypt's more recent but no less fascinating history.

"Guests will see the tombs of the workmen who actually built the pyramids and learn about how they lived and died," says Adriana Samluk, Quality Assurance Manager at Archaeological Paths. "Thanks to Dr Hawass, this site changed our concept of how the pyramids were built and he will be able to explain this first hand. It is an unparalleled insight into what Egypt is about."

www.archaeologicalpaths.com

Caribbean dreams

EAST WINDS ST LUCIA

East Winds a boutique resort in St Lucia that offers the authentic luxury Caribbean experience

"When you're at East Winds, you know that you're in St Lucia, not just in a random luxury hotel in a sunny part of the world," says Judith Milne, Director of the resort. "We are authentically Caribbean."

Set on a secluded beach within a quiet bay, East Winds, St Lucia is the Caribbean island's original boutique resort. A botanic garden by the sea, its 12 acres of land are filled with fertile plants and trees, its tranquil air disturbed only by a chorus of tropical birdsong.

Originally developed in the 1950s from rainforest, the resort now consists of 30 traditional cottage-style suites, as well as an ocean-front beach house, named Horlicks House, after the couple behind the bedtime drink, who once owned it.

"Guests can expect personalised care and all-inclusive service," says Milne. "You can lie in a hammock reading, go swimming in the very safe, quiet area off the beach, or get pampered in the garden spa by our therapist, using medicinal herbs and plants grown on site. If you're feeling more energetic, you can discover the rainforest, go out in a canoe or pedalo, learn to sail with our qualified instructors, go snorkelling, or enjoy dolphin and whale-watching. There's also a hiking trail with exercise points along the way, and an air-conditioned gym."

Dog lovers will be charmed by East Winds' own dog, Stanley, who was discovered, injured, as a new-born puppy during a rainstorm. "He's now been adopted," says Milne. "He's now a year old. He comes to work with me every day. He gets spoiled by the guests, gets to walk on the beach and swim in the sea. He's living the dream!"

The hotel has its own kitchen garden – produce from which is included in every meal – and a banana plantation. Meals are served in the beach restaurant, with accompaniment on a Steinway grand piano. While breakfast and lunch are casual affairs, evening dining is silver service, with multiple courses and a menu and wine list that change every night.

"The atmosphere here is exclusive, but very sociable," says Milne. "It has a colonial feel about it – a bit Agatha Christie, especially in the evenings. Everyone gathers in one lounge, for pre-dinner cocktails and champagne, and then they drift into a lovely candlelit dinner." It makes this Caribbean paradise a popular spot with honeymooners and wedding parties. Uniquely, East Winds gifts weddings to couples marrying in the resort. "We do all the legal arrangements, the cake, buttonholes, bouquet and so on, and donate the location," explains Milne.

Sustainability is important to East Winds. Milne's engineer husband has built a water-treatment plant, allowing the hotel to recycle its waste water. The hotel has banned plastic straws and is looking into replacing its energy generators with solar panels. Last year, East Winds started a family foundation to support the families of its 80 staff. "For us, the future is all about improving the lives of our team and the local community," says Milne. "We support lots of charities and local schools, and sponsor the local dogs home."

For Milne, the main appeal of East Winds is that it is a happy and sociable place. "Guests say they relax the minute they arrive. They instantly feel the stress and the strains melt away." *www.eastwinds.com*

Opposite: East Winds St Lucia mixes colonial-era luxury with an authentic Caribbean experience

Where East meets West

REIGNWOOD INVESTMENTS UK

Ten Trinity Square, in the heart of the City of London, is the Reignwood Group's luxury hotel and private club uniting East and West

Right: *Tony Truong, Head Chef at the contemporary Cantonese restaurant Mei Ume, one of two fine dining venues at Ten Trinity Square*

"Engaging leaders and thinkers across the world – from East to West and West to East – will enable the creation of a future that satisfies the needs of all," says Dr Chanchai Ruayrungruang, Chairman of Reignwood Group. This vision has informed the way that this Beijing-based company has lovingly renovated a grand and historic building in the heart of London. Behind its marble Corinthian columns, Ten Trinity Square provides a platform for leading figures in business, politics, academia, the performing and visual arts, and the professions to meet and greet in the financial district of the City of London.

This impressive Beaux Arts building near Tower Bridge has been given a new lease of life and a fresh decorative splendour thanks to the investment and care shown by Reignwood, which bought the former headquarters of the Port of London Authority near the Tower of London in 2010.

At the heart of the sensitive renovation is the Ten Trinity Square Private Club, a unique partnership between Reignwood Group, Four Seasons Hotels and Resorts and Château Latour. Situated in the boardrooms and executive offices of the original building, the club has been created as a global meeting place and a platform for business and cultural exchange. A collection of lavish yet discreet rooms provide space for conversation and relaxation. With hand-carved walnut panelling and high ornate ceilings, they include meeting rooms, a cigar sampling lounge, a bar, a billiards room and dining rooms. The club is also the world's first Château Latour Discovery Room outside France. Bronzed lighting and black-framed wine cellars are distinct features of the room, with some of Château Latour's most sought-after vintage wines on show.

"London's great clubs have traditionally played a vital role in shaping debate and facilitating exchange," says Dr Chanchai.

"Ten Trinity Square Private Club revives this proud tradition for a new, globalised era, at a time when London is establishing itself as the fulcrum between these two worlds of East and West."

Members are also able to take advantage of the unique partnership with three-Michelin-starred chef Anne-Sophie Pic in the Château Latour Dining Room.

Ten Trinity Square's Asian restaurant, Mei Ume, is named after a combination of the Japanese and Chinese words for "plum blossom" and, fittingly, specialises in carefully curated Chinese and Japanese dishes, including Peking duck, sushi and sashimi. The restaurant is overseen by Head Chef Tony Truong whose traditional Cantonese cooking has been learned through years working in Guangzhou.

The whole redevelopment has been comprehensively and meticulously restored and upgraded to ensure that it retains the detail and integrity of Sir Edwin Cooper's original 1922 building by preserving as many of the surviving features as possible. The building is also home to apartments, and a five-star Four Seasons Hotel.

The hotel, club and public areas have been designed by Parisian designers Bruno Moinard and Claire Bétaille of 4BI & Associés, renowned for combining the disciplines of creator and artist with a master craftsman's attention to detail. For Mei Ume, Ed Ng and Terence Ngan of AB Concept took inspiration from the building's heritage as a gateway for merchants from the East and West.

"The rebuilding of Ten Trinity Square was a long-term investment," says Dr Chanchai. "It is a key part of the Reignwood Group's vision and mission to promote business and cultural exchange between China, Asia and the West."
www.tentrinitysquare.com

CHAPTER SEVENTEEN

Leaders in learning
Education for everyone

From nursery schools to research universities, institutions around the world are sharing the Prince of Wales's beliefs about the benefits of a holistic education

The knowledge champion

A PRINCELY EDUCATION

With his Teaching Institute Schools Programme, his Education Summer Schools and The Prince's Trust, Prince Charles has made a commitment to education and training a key priority

For the Prince of Wales, education is linked to a nexus of natural wisdoms that encompass ecology, agriculture, science and religion. "It is about reminding people of what has been lost throughout the 20th century, and how we can recover a proper balance," he said in a 2004 speech at one of his Education Summer Schools in Buxton. "I often think that the kind of fashionable changes we have witnessed in the field of education during the last 50 years have been mirrored in other areas of life – in particular with regard to agriculture and the environment, architecture and certain aspects of healthcare: a move from an 'organic' approach... to a 'genetically modified' approach which cuts us off from our cultural and historical heritage and relies on ceaseless, clinical experimentation."

It is a subject close to his heart, and why the Prince set up his Teaching Institute Schools Programme and his Education Summer Schools, and also why he serves as a Patron of Teach First. Some of his beliefs have been labelled "traditionalist", and the Prince is certainly resistant to modern buzzwords in pedagogy, such as "learnacy", "learning managers" or "pupil-centred learning". While acknowledging the importance of "learning how to learn" it is the imparting of timeless knowledge that the Prince regards as key. "We owe it to the next generation to give bodies of knowledge to children," he says, "even though they may not necessarily appreciate or understand the need for such depth and breadth at an early stage."

The Prince is sceptical of justifying education on utilitarian grounds alone. "Education matters because it is through education that children discover their common humanity," he has said. "It is about opening people's minds; it is about exploration, discovery; about undertaking journeys." But he remains a strong advocate for vocational education,

something that has informed the expansion of his biggest charity project, The Prince's Trust.

"I have come to appreciate that many pupils who have an aptitude for vocational skills often experience low self-esteem because they can feel they are unable to engage with academic studies as well as others and are therefore sometimes stigmatised as preparing for 'second-rate' training and, eventually, jobs," he said in 2004. "Yet, how often does one hear about the dearth of skilled craftsmen in this country and the need to train more people? Everybody, in my view, has a talent of one sort or another, which is the premise on which I've tried to base the work of the Prince's Trust, but so often it needs the skills of parents and teachers to find them; to grow and to foster them."

Indeed, it is The Prince's Trust that might prove to be Charles's most impressive legacy. Founded in 1976, it supports people aged between 11 and 30, many of them from vulnerable backgrounds, including those leaving care or facing issues such as homelessness or problems with mental health. The Prince's Trust runs a range of training and educational programmes, each year helping more than 60,000 young people move on to employment, education, volunteering or training.

"We must find a way of ensuring that all young people understand that a vocational or craft-based job can be immensely satisfying," says the Prince, "and that this work is of equal value to an employer and society as a whole as work in administration, research or management. When I travel round the country meeting people from every sort of background, it is rare that I find skilled craftsmen or women who are unhappy in their work. They usually derive a real sense of satisfaction and, above all, pride from what they do."

Below: *The Prince of Wales addressing*
a reception for The Prince's Trust
in London, February 2018

Future-facing education

HORNSEY SCHOOL FOR GIRLS

The holistic approach of Hornsey School for Girls ensures that its students are well prepared for the future

Term is in full swing at Hornsey School for Girls in north London – but it is not all heads-down in the classroom. On any given day students across the school are involved in a range of activities and experiences that would have been unimaginable when the school was founded 130 years ago.

"This Tuesday our Year 7s – the youngest students at the school – are completely off-timetable, spending the whole day in enterprise workshops," says Angela Rooke, the school's acting Headteacher. "On Wednesday our Year 9s are taking part in a charity project where they have been twinned with children at a school in a refugee camp in Jordan. On Friday the National Theatre is coming into school to do a production of *The Curious Incident of the Dog in the Nighttime*. This is just a normal week."

The school's motto is "the better prepared, the stronger" and, for the staff, that means providing more than just academic excellence for all their students. They believe it is also the school's duty to empower their students with broader skills that will help them in the future. This holistic approach to education is paying off. The school scored a progress score of 0.66 in 2017, which means every student performed better than they were expected to at the start of the year. This was the highest progress score in the borough of Haringey.

"This is not an accident," says Rooke. "We have looked strategically at how children learn, and have put creative learning processes at the centre of everything we do. Whatever the subject, our teachers facilitate lessons and include problem solving, critical thinking, teamwork and using emotional intelligence to find a solution. In English lessons, that might mean delving deeper into a character in a story, or taking the original story down a different path, role-playing what might have happened differently. The ownership of learning lies with our students. We pick up on a young person's passion, whether that's music or dance or maths or technology. We see each and every child as an individual and adapt accordingly."

In recent years the school has been developing partnerships with local groups, businesses and organisations to give students a variety of insights and practical experiences into future career paths. All that the capital has to offer is on their doorstep. "We are in London, and we try to enable our students to experience the very best of the city," says Rooke. "We want to build wider aspirations in our students and open doors to them they have never even seen before. We are very fortunate that our students come from such a wide range of social and cultural backgrounds – we encourage them to explore possibilities that might not be accessible to them elsewhere. The diversity of our school community also provides opportunities for students to share their experience and learn from one another."

Sixth-form students are teamed up with mentors from various professions and industries such as law, business, medicine and even motor racing. Many mentors are women, to surround the students with as many positive female role models as possible.

"With technology changing so rapidly, we know the jobs many of our students are going to work in just don't exist yet," Rooke says. "But we open their eyes to what is possible, let them experience wider networks beyond the school itself and show them the bigger picture. Our passion is empowering our students to have high expectations of themselves, of what they can achieve, and of what the future holds for them."
www.hsg.haringey.sch.uk

"We have put creative learning processes at the centre of everything we do," says acting Headteacher Angela Rooke

Below: *The library building at the*
Marcus Family Campus of Ben-Gurion
University of the Negev

Desert wisdom

BEN-GURION UNIVERSITY OF THE NEGEV

Ben-Gurion University is an internationally renowned research institution that shares Prince Charles's environmental concerns

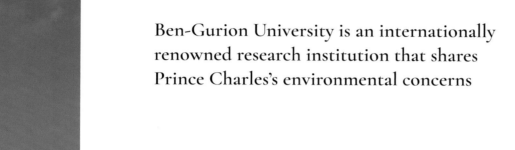

"The Prince of Wales has pioneered support for sustainability and the environment, and has been a great supporter of education, research and the arts all his life," says Professor Rivka Carmi, President of Ben-Gurion University of the Negev. "Like us he understands the value of supporting local communities and protecting the environment. Many of our programmes and research focus on these issues."

Ben-Gurion University of the Negev is one of Israel's leading public research universities, with around 20,000 students and 4,000 faculty members covering all major disciplines in engineering sciences, health sciences and natural sciences, as well as humanities, business and social sciences. More than 130,000 alumni play important roles in all areas of research and development, industry, healthcare, the economy, society, culture and education in Israel. Students and faculty hail from all parts of Israeli society, and daily life on campus brings together Jews, Christians, Muslims, Bedouins and Arab Israelis, as well as immigrants and exchange students from all over the world.

Israel has, by necessity, had to pioneer ways of running a first-world economy with very limited natural resources, and researchers at Ben-Gurion University have been among the great minds who made this possible. "With the increasing need for sources of water and food, I am sure the Prince would be fascinated to learn how we are developing ways to farm fish even in the desert, by purifying water that cannot be consumed by humans," says Professor Carmi. "We also use the same water for irrigation. Our research teams look for solutions to pressing problems in the world today." Indeed, the global revolution in water desalination was made possible by research on scaling up the reverse osmosis process carried out at the university's Blaustein Institutes for Desert Research.

The university has five campuses throughout the Negev Desert region: three, including the main campus, are in the city of Beer-Sheva (120 km south of both Tel Aviv and Jerusalem), a campus at Sede Boqer (40 km south of Beer-Sheva) and the Eilat campus (200 km further south, on the Red Sea). It is home to several multi-disciplinary research institutes, including the National Institute for Biotechnology in the Negev; the National Institute of Solar Energy; the Ilse Katz Institute for Nanoscale Science and Technology; the Jacob Blaustein Institutes for Desert Research; and the Ben-Gurion Research Institute for the Study of Israel & Zionism.

Through its technology-transfer company, BGN Technologies, which is also responsible for the university's patent portfolio, Ben-Gurion University initiates and implements projects with institutions, companies and foundations worldwide. It also attracts strategic partners and investors in the fields of science, technology and industry. Ben-Gurion University is a partner in the initiative and establishment of the Advanced Technologies Park: a hi-tech and biotechnology project located next to the university's Marcus Family Campus. This unique public–private partnership combines the outstanding achievements of the university with leading companies in Israel and worldwide.

The university prides itself on a commitment to the surrounding communities, with over a third of its students participating in community action programmes. Its commitment to sustainability is evident in its "Green Campus" initiative, and Ben-Gurion ranked 46th in the world rankings of universities with sustainable policies. It is also developing curricula for a wide range of undergraduate and graduate degrees in the fields of energy – something that the Prince would surely approve of. *in.bgu.ac.il/en*

Sound advice

BRITISH INTERNATIONAL SCHOOL WROCŁAW

For British International School Wrocław co-founder
Andy Harris music is both a personal passion and
a means of nurturing creative thought

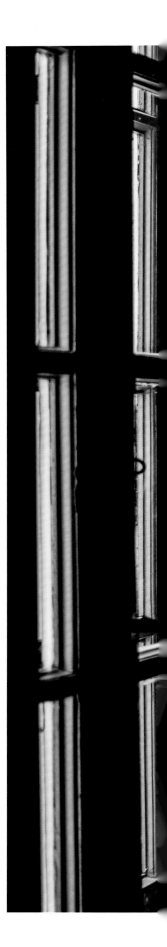

Musician and composer Andy Harris has spent a lifetime inspiring children to play music, but he didn't particularly enjoy his own piano lessons as a child. "It was only when I started tinkering around on my own, making up my own music, that I realised how incredible it was," he says. "I absolutely fell in love with composing." Driven by this passion, Harris has enjoyed an extraordinary career both in education and creating music.

Originally from Worcester, Harris grew up surrounded by music thanks to his opera-loving parents. After leaving college he fell into teaching as a temporary stop-gap in his music writing career. But when he took a job as head of music at a school in Staffordshire he found himself enthralled with the challenge.

"I built up an orchestra at the school but the children needed music to play," he says. "So I began to compose music specifically for children. To write music for their ability, so they could get really involved in what they were performing, was so rewarding." His notable extended works from this time were the recorder ensemble piece "Jazzin' Around" and a musical for children, *Pinocchio*, which was performed at the Gatehouse Theatre in Staffordshire.

In 1992, seeking a new challenge in life, he moved to Poland, fascinated by a country that was going through major change after the end of communism. Harris began teaching at an international school in Warsaw and was then asked to help set up and run a new international school in Krakow. Two further schools in Wrocław and Łódź followed as expatriate communities in Poland began to grow.

"The schools we have created are very special places," says Harris. "We have small class sizes, which makes a huge difference when you are teaching something like music. We really want to develop each child to their maximum potential, beyond what even their parents would expect. The child is the centre of everything we do."

He resumed his work composing for children, writing songs and instrumental pieces for plays and English-language learning materials, and getting the children at his schools to record voice parts and perform songs. "Writing music for children is not easy but it is so valuable," he says. "I know children who have learned English through the songs that I have written."

He also continued his classical compositions. "For me, writing a piece of music starts with a concept. One composition, 'Cloudscape', came from watching the movement of clouds across the sky from my balcony. I wrote another, 'Parallel Lines', mostly on the train when I was commuting between Warsaw and Kraków. I saw the railway journey as an analogy for human interactions – the way the tracks converge and break apart like our relationships can do. So the music developed thematically from that."

At the end of this academic year, in summer 2019, Harris is leaving the classroom behind to concentrate solely on composing. "Being in education is one of the greatest privileges anyone can have," he says. "Looking back at all the children who have been through our schools and gone on to university – it's very humbling to have been a part of that. It has shaped me as a composer. Now I am lucky enough to be able to focus on writing the kind of music I want to write. Education has given my musical creativity its freedom."

andyharris.eu • bisc.wroclaw.pl

*Educator and composer
Andy Harris*

Fluent delivery

L'ECOLE DES PETITS & L'ECOLE DE BATTERSEA

L'Ecole des Petits in Fulham and L'Ecole de Battersea have pioneered bilingual education in London, winning the acclaim of British and French education systems

Opposite: "We are described as 'the most British of the French schools in London'," says founder Mirella Otten

"The beauty of starting early is that you have pretty much a blank sheet of paper to work with, so whatever your nationality is, or whichever language you speak at home, it is easier," says Nick Otten, co-founder of L'Ecole des Petits and L'Ecole de Battersea. "If your child only speaks one language with you and you give him or her a bilingual education, this can help them acquire an additional language as part of a natural process."

L'Ecole des Petits (which takes children aged 3–6) and L'Ecole de Battersea (for children aged 3–11) are two partnered bilingual schools in south-west London, both of which have been ranked "Outstanding" by Ofsted. L'Ecole des Petits was established in 1977 by Mirella Otten, initially working out of a church hall in Chelsea before moving to a refurbished Victorian building in Fulham in 1991. It was the first UK independent pre-primary school to provide a structured bilingual nursery education based on the French "école maternelle" system.

In the late 1970s bilingual schools were rare in the UK, but the success of L'Ecole des Petits led it to be the first early-years school in the UK to be accredited by the Agency for French Education Abroad as an "école homologuée" in 1995. As demand grew from parents, Mirella opened a second school, L'Ecole de Battersea, in 2005, expanding the age range to cover pre-primary and primary.

Mirella grew up in a bilingual French/Italian household before marrying Nick, an Englishman, and her pan-European background has led her to attach an importance to bilingualism. "Aged three, a child's mind is like a sponge," she says. "It can more easily absorb new information presented to it than an older child and therefore is better equipped to assimilate a second language. The younger the child, the easier it is."

Despite this bilingual environment, Mirella's schools have a strong commitment to British culture, mixing the structured academic methodology of the French educational system with British values, sensitivity, creativity and imagination. "We are described as 'the most British of the French schools in London' in *Tatler Schools Guide 2019*, and so we are," says Mirella. "When you come to live in another country, you must adapt to new customs, culture and language. This allows you to understand the people around you, all the while keeping your own identity."

This approach is a fundamental pillar of the school, which welcomes over 30 different nationalities. "We are non-selective," says Mirella. "All children should have the same chances whatever their background, and while they will all evolve differently, they should all have the opportunity to progress to the best of their ability, and to be encouraged to do so."

"We always strive to evolve," says Nick, "with constant self-questioning and looking for ways to improve and be progressive while at the same time maintaining our strong traditional values and culture."

The school is delighted to celebrate Prince Charles's 70th birthday. "We have long admired his fine work in setting up and running the Prince's Trust to provide opportunities for young people, which is surely an inspiration to us all, young and old alike," says Nick. "To provide an equal opportunity to all young people through education from the earliest of ages is so important, and this underlies our philosophy at L'Ecole des Petits and L'Ecole de Battersea, as it also underlies His Royal Highness's many benevolent and supportive activities."
www.lecoledespetits.co.uk

Shared knowledge

UNIVERSITY COLLEGE SCHOOL, HAMPSTEAD

University College School fosters strong links with London state schools, extending the reach of its outstanding liberal education

"We go about our business in an informal yet purposeful way to develop independent individuals, and seek to share our distinctive style of education with as many young people as possible," says Mark Beard, Headmaster of University College School (UCS). UCS was founded in 1830, offering a liberal education inspired by the ideas of the philosopher Jeremy Bentham. Today, as a member of the Eton Group of 14 independent schools in England, it achieves outstanding results in a competitive, stimulating environment.

While unashamedly academic, the school's culture is strongly influenced by its community work. "My role is to make the school as porous as possible to the local community," says Assistant Head Edward Roberts. "Almost all our sixth-form pupils are involved in our Partnership Programme as classroom assistants or helping to run school clubs." He is justifiably proud of the commitment that drives staff and pupils to offer their time, skills and fundraising ingenuity to schools and charities in London and overseas.

This includes long-established partnerships with the London Academy of Excellence (LAE) in Stratford and Westminster Academy, with Beard sitting on both governing bodies. "Our work with LAE includes reciprocal student visits to lessons and collaborative projects," says Beard. "We also have three teachers working there and absolutely loving it; another teaches Latin at Westminster Academy."

When UCS launched a 40-minute maths breakfast club for a local school, the response was typically enthusiastic. "I presented this in assembly, explaining that pupils would need to get to the school for 8am, that they had to submit a proper written application and then be assessed," says Roberts. "I still got 36 applications for 16 places." When pupils from partner schools come to university applications, UCS invites them to support evenings. "Students preparing for medical interviews, for example, will be put through a whole carousel of questions, with interviewers also being sourced from UCS parents. For those applying to Oxbridge for STEM (science, technology, engineering, maths) subjects, we give mock interviews and feedback."

Besides academic support, UCS also makes sports and drama facilities available. "Last year we invited a dozen pupils from Westminster Academy to use our swimming pool for an intensive course," says Roberts. UCS ran chemistry and modern-language immersion mornings for primary school pupils, as well as inviting 200 pupils to a performance of *The Tempest*. UCS also works with the Sir Hubert Von Herkomer Foundation, running digital photography courses that are attended by pupils from two partnership schools.

"UCS parents are conscious of the place in the community that the school holds," explains Roberts, "and wholeheartedly support the school's fundraising initiatives, which involve the whole school throughout November and December. Pupils pick the charities and devise their own money-raising activities. They might raise £2,000 or only £2.50, but their efforts are all celebrated at the end of term."

The school outreach programme includes an annual trip to work with a charity in Goa, taking a specially selected group of eight upper-sixth pupils to work with orphans and street children. "Predominantly they are there to play with the children," says Roberts. "These are youngsters who simply don't know how to play." For 15 years, the school has also had links in Romania, where 40 students work for two weeks during their summer holiday.

Whether overseas or closer to home, the pupils and staff at UCS are energetically involved in sharing their knowledge, experience and time. "Our pupils go out to benefit the community and in turn the benefits come back to them."
www.ucs.org.uk

Below: *Working closely with other local schools and community projects has reaped rewards for the pupils at UCS in north London*

A roaring success

DRAGON SCHOOL

Originally set up to educate the sons of Oxford dons, Dragon School is now a progressive co-educational prep school with a strong sense of community

Dragon School has evolved with a belief that a school should do more than simply provide an outstanding all-round education. This Oxford prep school also has a commitment to social impact that has informed its outlook for more than a century.

"One of our earliest head teachers, Charles 'Skipper' Lynam, modernised the school and believed in developing a social conscience among the children," explains current Head Dr Crispin Hyde-Dunn. "We still encourage, facilitate and coordinate these opportunities for children to make a difference in the world, both locally and globally. Our Dragon values are kindness, courage and respect. These values are at the very heart of what it means to be a Dragon and we feel they are values that chime with the Prince's life's work."

Indeed, when Prince Charles visited the school in 2004, the occasion was solemn but also illustrative of the school's commitment to loyalty, internationalism and social values. His Royal Highness was unveiling a plaque dedicated to former Dragon pupil Nicholas Knatchbull, the Prince's godson, who was killed by the IRA in 1979 alongside his grandfather Earl Mountbatten, who was also a mentor and godfather to Charles.

"We now have the Knatchbull Trust, a bursary scheme run by Nicholas's twin brother, Tim," says Dr Hyde-Dunn. "There's also a Nicholas Knatchbull Travel Fund offering financial assistance to former pupils, known as Old Dragons, who want to travel with a focus on helping communities abroad. The affection and respect in which the Dragon is held by former former pupils and staff is phenomenal." Trips funded by the Nicholas Knatchbull Travel Fund include assisting at an orphanage in Morocco and teaching English to the street children of Ecuador.

The Dragon was founded in 1877, originally for the sons of Oxford University dons, and evolved rapidly under "Skipper" Lynam in the first half of the 20th century. It is now a co-ed with more than 800 day and boarding pupils aged 4 to 13. The school prides itself on nurturing individuals and offering a wide-ranging curriculum, but is also characterised by a strong sense of community. It is international in outlook: as well as local children, overseas pupils come from more than two dozen countries. Exchange trips take them to places such as Tokyo and New York and the school also receives strong support from parents and Old Dragons throughout the world.

The school benefits from its location in the university city of Oxford. There are strong links between the school and the surrounding colleges through governors and local parents, many of whom are academics and choose Dragon School for its all-round education. "We can tap into everything Oxford has to offer, including the world-class museums and many of the various academic faculties," says Dr Hyde-Dunn. "We are very privileged to be part of such an exciting and inspiring landscape."

Former pupils are as diverse as actor and campaigner Emma Watson and the Metropolitan Police Commissioner Cressida Dick. This demonstrates the range of talents that the school can help develop. "We attract bright, capable, engaged families and then we add value," says Dr Hyde-Dunn. "We find the skills and talents within every child and we promote and develop them through the school in a vibrant, energetic and forward-thinking environment. We are always looking to help pupils think about where they can make a difference with local, national and global issues."

www.dragonschool.org

Faith in education

CONVENT OF JESUS AND MARY LANGUAGE COLLEGE

The Convent of Jesus and Mary Language College
is using traditional educational principles to teach
modern, urban Londoners

On a quiet street, hidden away behind high walls and surrounded by exquisite gardens, the Convent of Jesus and Mary Language College is located only yards away from the bustle and noise of Willesden in north-west London. "Coming here really is like stepping into a spiritual haven," says Headmistress Louise McGowan.

The school was established 130 years ago by a group of French nuns from the RJM (the Religious of Jesus and Mary), a Catholic religious order established by St Claudine Thevenet following the French Revolution. "Her mission was to educate orphaned children as a way out of poverty," explains McGowan. "There are now Convents of Jesus and Mary in 28 different countries, many of them in the Commonwealth. We are a very strong international community of both religious sisters and lay people, like myself."

Based in the Borough of Brent, the 1,000-pupil, single-sex secondary school reflects its multi-ethnic and multi-faith catchment, accepting girls from all religions and from secular backgrounds. However, it is strongly grounded in Catholicism, both in practice and in ethos, with Mass held twice a week, and observance of feast days. "Our charism dates back to the original work of St Claudine," says McGowan. "We see God in everything and everyone. We see the image of God in every child, in their spirits and their unique gifts, and we aim to draw these out while at the same time providing them with the highest-quality education. Brent is an area with a lot of poverty and deprivation, and education is the springboard for our pupils to become the young women they're meant to be."

The school's culture of achievement – which encompasses a focus on music, drama, dance and the visual arts, as well as academic subjects – has seen many of its girls go on to study at Oxbridge and Russell Group universities. Its Fulbright Scholarship programme also allows two or three girls each year to go to the United States to study.

With pupils from all over the world, there are many languages spoken at the school. All pupils are offered the opportunity to study French, Spanish and Italian, and they can also choose to take qualifications in their home language, with children learning Portuguese, Arabic, Urdu, Russian and Polish, among others. "We promote languages and encourage the children to be proud of their own cultural heritage, which enriches our community here," says McGowan.

The Convent of Jesus and Mary, which regularly wins the International School Award, has just entered into a partnership with Steinway & Sons, making it the first state school in the UK to have a full-sized grand piano in its assembly hall. McGowan plans to invite professional musicians and students from music colleges to come to perform recitals, bringing "high-end music culture" to the girls; something that many of them would not have the chance to access normally. The school has also just become the first Centre for Research in Catholic Education in the south east of England.

"All of these things really help to put our school on the map," says McGowan. "I see my job as my vocation, and my mission is to ensure the best possible education and opportunities for my pupils, regardless of their ability and backgrounds. In the future, I want the name of the Convent of Jesus and Mary on everybody's lips. We are going to produce some quite wonderful young women."

www.cjmlc.co.uk

The Convent of Jesus and Mary
Language College provides its pupils
with a window to the world

Below: *Pupils at Ark Boulton Academy are taught the importance of giving something back to their local community*

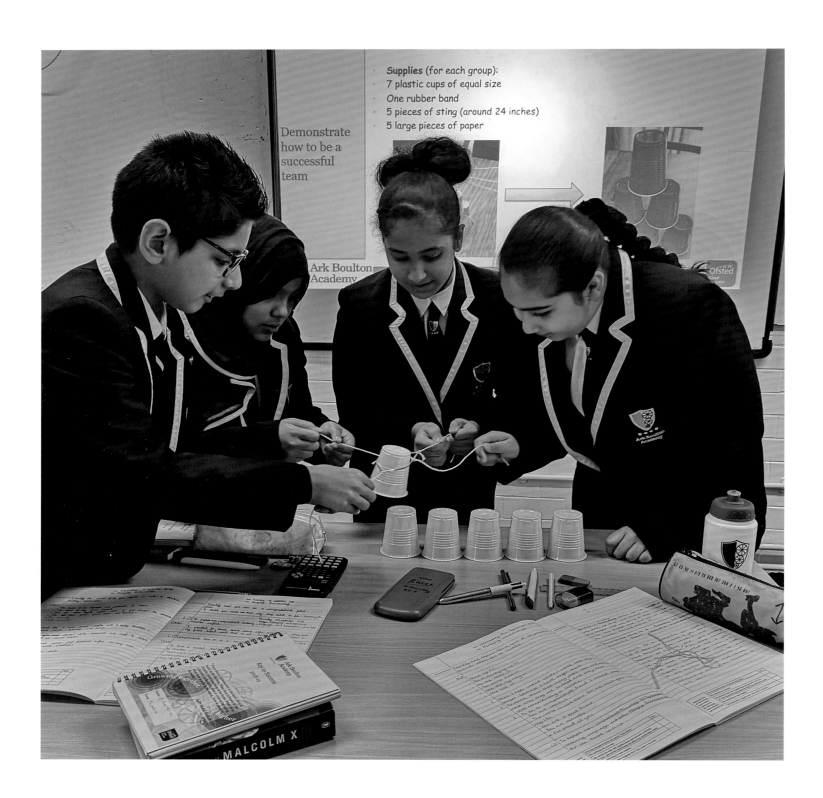

Growing together

ARK BOULTON ACADEMY

Ark Boulton Academy in Birmingham shows how a failing inner-city school can be transformed into a beacon of excellence

"It takes a whole community to bring up a child," explains Herminder Channa, Principal and educational trailblazer behind the newly reformed Ark Boulton Academy in the Sparkbrook area of Birmingham. "*In loco parentis* is the phrase I always use to summarise our understanding of what it means to be a teacher in the 21st century."

Yet the school – which is locally renowned for its values, curriculum of compassion, tolerance, respect, self-discipline, charity, justice, honesty, courage, service and commitment – wasn't always such a glowing beacon of educational ideals. Channa, a qualified teacher and lead Ofsted inspector, took the helm in 2015 at a time when the school was in special measures and had a number of investigative hearings pending.

"It was a tough school that had been struggling for years and had a high turnover of senior management," Channa remembers. "Educationally speaking, it was very unstable: students were joining us from 33 different feeder schools and 65 per cent of staff were supply because we had such bad retention. When I began formulating our mission statement and planning how we were going to turn things around, I had to be sensitive to what the community had been through previously. Parents were very upset, which is understandable – their children's education had been badly disrupted."

The key priority was to rebuild trust. "I knew that we needed to get the community back on board," says Channa. "It was about making ourselves visible to parents and staff, and hearing their concerns."

Three years on, the transformation of this deprived inner-city school is unprecedented. Ark Boulton now boasts the highest secondary attendance in a network of 38 schools and has achieved an incredible 95 per cent staff retention rate. Yet Channa's vision is about more than quantifiable success.

"The most important lesson students will learn at Ark Boulton is that they are part of something bigger," she says. "We aim to teach them that they have a responsibility to the community in which they live. Part one of our mission statement is that every child will go on to university or be able to access a career or apprenticeship of their choice, but part two is that each student will use this experience to upskill their local community, to look after their parents and become a role model to their younger siblings. To me, academic excellence means nothing if it isn't in service to others."

Yet in an area of such high deprivation, the inevitable challenge remains of plugging the cultural deficit and helping students to feel connected to the wider society in which they live. "Young people need to feel like they are part of making modern Britain, which is why we created Pledge Days," Channa explains. "It's our promise to the students of Ark Boulton that we will take them somewhere twice per year they've never been before, whether that's St Paul's Cathedral or the great British seaside."

Channa's vision of positivity and inclusivity is infectious. By the example of her own leadership, staff at the school are encouraged to espouse the values curriculum through their own behaviour and teaching. "It's about being authentic role models," she says. "As leaders, we need to demonstrate to our students what forgiveness looks like – what resilience looks like. If we can produce a younger generation who understand their civic duty and create a more tolerant community, then it's a job well done." *arkboulton.org*

Learning for life

NOCN

NOCN provides qualifications, assessments and training that improves the employability of hundreds of thousands of people each year

When NOCN – formally known as the National Open College Network – was founded 30 years ago as a charity, it concentrated on providing the basic English and maths skills that the unemployed needed to get into work. These days, its remit is far wider. NOCN now delivers qualifications and assessments for around 700,000 people each year in the UK and abroad as it helps train people at every educational stage, from entry level to Level 7, in the process partnering with organisations such as the Prince's Trust.

"The problem now isn't unemployment, it is zero-hours contracts and gig work," explains Managing Director Graham Hasting-Evans. "There is low unemployment, but this work is not always sustainable. That's why we've moved on from those basic courses that get somebody on the ladder and have gone further, which has taken us to degree level and beyond. We need to show people a career path that is sustainable and helps them achieve their aspirations."

Hastings-Evans likens NOCN to organisations such as City & Guilds and Pearson Edexcel, who provide vocational and further education qualifications. NOCN works across multiple sectors, providing educational opportunities at all levels. Courses can be taught on the job, in classrooms and increasingly over the internet, with some management courses now delivered entirely online.

But NOCN was founded as a charity to combat the issues of deprivation and unemployment in the 1980s, and that attitude still shapes the direction of their work. The organisation's parent body was the Learning And Work Institute, whose patron is Princess Anne, a charity that supports adult education through research and campaigning, and NOCN itself takes a proactive approach and one committed to diversity. They seek out people in all communities who would benefit from further qualification.

"What makes us unique among the awarding organisations is that we do more diverse things to get people into employment than simply offer awards," says Hasting-Evans. "And we are the only one that has Leaders In Diversity status from the National Centre For Diversity. A large proportion of our learners come from disadvantaged backgrounds, and we help those who genuinely need it. We do this for all people, whether people are disabled, different genders, different ethnicity, different religions – all the groups you can imagine. That's what we are about, helping get people into work and doing well in work. It's important to do practical things, such as set up the course so there are no barriers for entry, but we also work with charitable organisations such as the Prince's Trust to positively engage people. We go out and seek to effect change through political engagement and lobbying as well as the day-to-day work of offering certificates."

The organisation has been heavily involved in the rolling out of new apprenticeships having helped deliver some of the pilot schemes such as the steel fixing apprenticeship and it is continuing to work extensively in this area. NOCN is even taking it abroad. "Overseas, we are about to do some work with India taking the idea of the British apprenticeships to India, where they don't usually learn on the job," he says. "The Indian government wants to bring this idea of skilling to India, and we are working on that with the UK and Indian governments to deliver courses in banking and construction."

www.nocn.org.uk

NOCN's qualifications and assessments help thousands into meaningful employment each year

Below: *Fourah Bay College has been educating West Africa's finest students since 1827*

A beacon of learning

FOURAH BAY COLLEGE, SIERRA LEONE

The oldest university in West Africa, Fourah Bay College has been an academic magnet for Commonwealth students for nearly two centuries

Known as "the Athens of West Africa" thanks to the crucial role it has played in educating students from Nigeria, Ghana, the Gambia, Cameroon, Namibia, South Africa and beyond, Fourah Bay College in Freetown, Sierra Leone has established a prestigious reputation among the continent's academic institutions. And, as the college approaches its bicentenary in 2027, Professor Joe Alie, Dean of the School of Postgraduate Studies, believes the country's change of government could signal a bright future for this beacon of learning.

"Since the elections in Sierra Leone earlier this year there has been a strengthening commitment to the future of the university, particularly from the newly created Ministry of Technical and Higher Education," explains Professor Alie.

Vice Chancellor Professor Foday Sahr is also very hopeful. "We've had a series of meetings with the Minister and other government officials, and the support from their side is very promising," he says. "So despite some of the challenges, I feel very optimistic about our future. I think over the next two or three years we will see a lot of progress in areas such as funding, the recruitment of lecturers, and improvements to facilities."

Historically, the college certainly has an impressive track record in meeting and overcoming challenges. Having unsuccessfully tried to establish a Christian institution in nearby Regent in the early 1800s, the Christian Missionary Society (CMS) returned to the idea with the launch of the college at Fourah Bay, in the east end of Freetown, in 1827. The college grew rapidly, with sizeable new facilities opened in 1848, but mounting financial pressures saw it close just a decade later. The college's fortunes were revived in 1870 by Rev Metcalfe Sunter, who succeeded in affiliating Fourah Bay College to Durham University in the UK, and the institution was able to grant its first degrees in 1879. Once again the college flourished, and as part of its development a foundation stone for a new science building was laid in April 1925 by the Prince of Wales.

The Sierra Leone government assumed full responsibility for Fourah Bay College from CMS in 1954, and the range of courses increased substantially, with degree courses in civil, mechanical and electrical engineering introduced in 1965. In 1967 the affiliation with Durham University ended and the college became the core constituent part of the University of Sierra Leone.

Having survived the ravages of the civil war, the college now has around 10,000 enrolled students, and today offers graduate and postgraduate courses across five faculties – applied accounting, arts, engineering, pure and applied sciences, and social sciences and law. However, Professor Alie recognises that success brings with it new challenges. "As the number of students grows, a lot of our faculties are reaching capacity, and staffing levels are becoming stretched," he says. "So the challenge now is to improve and increase the facilities such as laboratories, libraries, and lecture and seminar rooms, as well as recruiting more staff who are committed to the university's future.

"The government's stronger commitment to financial support – as the university's main funder – is an important step. It would be great if we could encourage overseas academic staff – particularly at the graduate level – to come and teach at the university, even for short periods of time such as a sabbatical or a postgraduate study break or placement. That's something we're working on now. We already have a number of exchanges in place with other universities, both in Africa and overseas, and the future for the university is looking very positive."
www.usl.edu.sl

Hearts, minds and hands

ST JOHN'S UNIVERSITY OF TANZANIA

St John's University of Tanzania is a centre
of academic excellence that strives to impart
a spirit of service in its students

"The shared ambition at St John's University of Tanzania is to be a Christian university of global standards," says Vice Chancellor Professor Emmanuel Mbennah. From its humble beginnings as an Anglican school founded by a missionary bishop, the Rt Rev Alfred Stanway, in the mid-1950s, St John's has transformed itself into a leading university that has produced almost 10,000 graduates to date at certificate, diploma, bachelors degree and masters degree levels.

"Our three strongest bachelor's programmes – pharmacy, science education and nursing – are viewed by many as the best in the country," says Professor Mbennah. "Our schools of pharmacy and nursing are the largest in terms of enrolment, and we have several prestigious masters programmes including business studies, education and theology. Our reputation is such that our graduates have a real advantage when it comes to being employed before the graduates of other institutions. We command respect and receive very strong commendations from government, employers and the church. Even the President of Tanzania has praised St John's University and approved our good work!"

Yet the key lesson that St John's students learn is one that cannot be measured academically. "The most important lesson that our students come away with, beyond the excellent education itself, is that the purpose of education is the transformation of the student, equipping them for the service of others," says Professor Mbennah. "There is no greater motivation to pursue an education than this. This philosophy is built into our founding principles and expressed through our motto, 'to learn to serve'."

It is precisely this faith-based ideology that makes the university unique, and drives its commitment to the highest possible standards of education. "Our vision of education is not just the acquisition of knowledge, but the transformation of the individual," says Professor Mbennah. "Through the rigorous education we provide, we want to make our students eager to serve others in whatever field they study, and to embrace this spirit of service and sacrifice that is at the heart of the Christian faith. We believe in education as something not just for the mind and brain, but also for the heart and hands. A holistic education is about so much more than obtaining a certificate; students are not simply customers at the university: they are valued co-creators of what we do and stakeholders in our mission."

Motivated by this commitment to a holistic education and inspired by his faith, Professor Mbennah is ambitious for the school. "We are very keen to increase student numbers from the current 5,300 to 10,000 or 12,000. Parents want their children to live safely on campus to focus on their academic, social and spiritual development, so we need more accommodation, more lecture theatres, and more office space. We also plan to construct a modern library with books and journals available online."

As well as outlining various doctoral programmes he wishes to introduce, Professor Mbennah is also determined to personally introduce a curriculum to professionalise people who work with vulnerable children. "St John's University is using a campus that was originally designed as a high school, so we need more facilities to expand," he says. "We invite all those who are keen to invest in education to visit us, partner with us, and support us as we become a significant global player in the provision of quality university education for the betterment of our world."

www.sjut.ac.tz

Below: *Part of the Administration Block at the Chief Mazengo Campus in Dodoma, Tanzania*

Below: *An instructor and students during a training session in the Electrics Laboratory at the FESTO Authorised and Certified Training (FACT) Centre – the largest and most diverse of its kind in the world*

On course for success

CARIBBEAN MARITIME UNIVERSITY

The Caribbean Maritime University has become one of the world's top places to study the logistics, engineering and ecology of maritime issues

With campuses across the island of Jamaica and a commitment to sustainability, the Caribbean Maritime University (CMU) embodies two of the values cherished most deeply by HRH Prince Charles – the environment and the Commonwealth. President Fritz Pinnock outlines the university's remarkable achievements, explaining how the CMU is the sort of fast-moving establishment that is needed in the modern era, where development is so rapid. "We are very aggressive, forward thinking and agile in the way we develop a course and bring it to market very quickly," he says. "The Prince is looking at the Commonwealth to lead these changes, and we represent that freshness in education that he is looking for."

The Caribbean Maritime University was founded in 1980 as a joint project between Norway and Jamaica. It began with 30 students, who were trained to crew Jamaica's merchant ships. Now the university has more than 6,000 students who study in numerous areas related to maritime issues, from logistics and engineering to ecology, immigration, customs and cybersecurity. Students come to Jamaica not just from across the Caribbean, but from all over the world – from Asia, Africa, the Americas and Europe. The university also has close connections with UK universities and offers a variety of professional certificates accredited by British institutions.

CMU is the fast-growing university in the region. Pinnock puts this success partly down to the university being new and therefore free of many of the strictures that can inhibit older institutions. "We look at education from the perspective of the market, which means we look at where the jobs are and then work backwards to build our programme," he explains. "As a result, almost 90 per cent of our students get a job within six months of leaving the university. It's estimated that 60 per cent of the best jobs in the next decade haven't been invented yet, so we are training people for lifelong learning. Degrees alone do not make you employable, so we train for employment skills as well as professional certificates. That makes us very forward facing for the new generation of jobs."

The university's radical, market-led approach has seen it advise and collaborate with Caribbean governments, who are keen to improve the region's educational offerings. "We are teaching the governments of the Caribbean how to modernise education, by bringing educational and training strands together," says Pinnock. "We have a project working with youths from the inner city, training them in the skills they need – how to dive, how to handle a boat, how to grow oysters."

CMU's courses straddle every area from professional qualifications to doctorates. These operate within what Pinnock describes as the "blue economy", working in the space where land meets sea. "In the Caribbean, our water space is 20 times the size of the land space," he says. "That has huge potential, as well as environmental issues. We are looking to restore the Kingston Harbour, the world's seventh largest natural harbour, and the 90 per cent of coral reefs in Jamaica that have died. We are looking at a lot of issues around sustainability and have received national and international awards, such as the North American Environment Protection Award in 2018, which we won ahead of all North American universities. We take our responsibilities very seriously and are changing the landscape of education in the Caribbean."

srs.cmu.edu.jm

Masters of nursing

CANADIAN NURSES ASSOCIATION

The high standards championed by the
Canadian Nurses Association help explain
why Canada values its nurses so much

Canadians hold their nurses in very high regard. When the first stamp in Canadian history to feature a health theme was introduced, in 1958, it showed a nurse, wearing the traditional cap. In study after study, the Canadian people place nurses at the top of their list of most trusted professionals.

It's thanks in no small part to the efforts of the Canadian Nurses Association (CNA), which celebrates its 110th birthday in 2018. "In a federation of 13 little countries, which is really what Canada is, we have managed to create a profession that the public trusts above everybody else," says Michael Villeneuve, Chief Executive Officer of CNA.

"We've achieved that by having a common code of ethics, a common entry-to-practice exam, and a common curriculum. You must have a bachelor's degree in nursing to be a registered nurse, and you must have a master's degree to be a nurse practitioner. As a result, whether you're in northern Saskatchewan or Toronto, when you show up in the Emergency Room, you can expect to receive a certain level of care. That standard didn't just fall out of the sky – all of that infrastructure is built by professional associations."

CNA has grown and evolved enormously in its 110 years and received the honour of the Queen's patronage in 1957. "The organisation began before nurses were registered, when anybody could hang a sign on their door and say they were a nurse," says Villeneuve. "In the early days, CNA fulfilled the need for affiliation, which we still do today. But it also brought nurses together, in a country that has six time zones, that is large and very under-populated, so they didn't feel quite so alone." Back then, Villeneuve explains, nursing was largely a home-based private care business, with just a few charitable hospitals for the poor: today, two-thirds of CNA's 139,000 members – across all 13 of Canada's provinces and territories – work in hospitals.

Since its inception, CNA has been heavily influenced by the British nursing tradition. Its first president Mary Agnes Snively ("the mother of Canadian nursing") was among the first nurses in the world to receive training grounded in Florence Nightingale's principles.

"CNA's job originally was to help organise the education and regulation of nurses, to protect the public, to set the conditions for workplaces and pay, to lay down a bed of research," Villeneuve explains. "Over the years, nursing unions have evolved to take on the workplace and labour matters, and the Canadian Association of Schools of Nursing now oversees the education side."

In 2018 then, CNA is left with three key areas of work: laying down the principles of professional best practice, building strong leadership, and influencing policy through advocacy.

"If you stand back and look at the nursing profession, it got to where it is today through the hard work of groups like CNA and the Royal College of Nursing in the UK," says Villeneuve. "These associations are like the foundations of a house; they keep the house standing no matter how much the décor changes over the years. We've structured a profession that's seen as trustworthy, providing safe and reliable care, and that's brought enormous value to Canadians – and, through our international work, to the rest of the world."
www.cna-aiic.ca

Janice Rae, RN, MN, has devoted her career to better management of acute pain. The clinical nurse specialist is a member of the Acute Pain Service team at Foothills Medical Centre in Calgary, Alberta

Below: *A sixth-form student joins infant school students in a reading circle, one of Ghana International School's initiatives to build leadership skills and foster intergenerational understanding*

Lessons in legacy

GHANA INTERNATIONAL SCHOOL

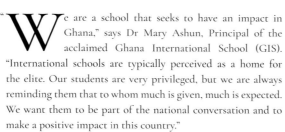

Established in 1955, Ghana International School
ensures that its students leave with a sense of duty
to their country and the wider world

"We are a school that seeks to have an impact in Ghana," says Dr Mary Ashun, Principal of the acclaimed Ghana International School (GIS). "International schools are typically perceived as a home for the elite. Our students are very privileged, but we are always reminding them that to whom much is given, much is expected. We want them to be part of the national conversation and to make a positive impact in this country."

To demonstrate how serious she and the rest of the senior leadership team are about impact, Dr Ashun has formally inscribed it into the school's five-year strategic plan. "As the oldest international school in Ghana, and one with a rich diplomatic history, we feel we have a great responsibility to the country and community in which we live," she explains. "We try to expose our students as much as possible to those who are less privileged, and we encourage them to have a positive attitude towards helping others."

These initiatives include a number of school charitable fundraising events, such as the annual sponsored walk for staff, students and parents, which this year raised around $30,000. "The focus of this event is to raise money for mental health awareness," says Dr Ashun. "The money we've raised has refurbished a mental health facility, provided mental health educational opportunities, and the discussion has helped to educate our children on how to recognise wellness in themselves and others."

Each year, the school also raises a considerable sum for the Children's Heart Foundation Ghana, which pays for the heart surgeries of those children who would not otherwise be able to afford it. "Each year we sponsor at least one child," says Dr Ashun. "Last year we were able to sponsor four heart surgeries, which is incredible. The students were delighted to be involved, as they saw this opportunity to save another child's life through their own fundraising efforts."

Yet Dr Ashun is firm in the opinion that student impact should also be about helping others in a sustainable way, not just donating money. "We often invite students from local schools where they don't have science facilities, so that our teachers and students can assist them to learn using the equipment in our laboratories," she says. "It's an opportunity for us to share our educational privilege with others." This regular collaboration with other schools and community outreach work is also an opportunity for GIS students to live out the values of the school and build mutual understanding.

"Our school runs a prefect system and we have classroom monitors, so there are many opportunities for students to hold positions of responsibility and leadership," Dr Ashun continues. "I was interviewing the newly elected Junior Boy's Prefect last week on what his campaign policies were, and he answered: 'I want every student to know that whatever they want to be, it's still special'. I thought that was such a beautiful sentiment.

"Academic results are one thing – our students achieve excellent grades and go on to study at the very best institutions – but our role has changed over time," Dr Ashun concludes. "We have gone from being simply an excellent place of education, to one that has a legacy and is impactful: one that constantly asks itself, 'what have you left behind to make the world better for everyone else?' That is one of the most important lessons I hope our students will learn."

www.gis.edu.gh

Prince Charles's official titles

WHAT EACH TITLE MEANS

His full official title is: His Royal Highness Prince Charles Philip Arthur George, Prince of Wales, KG, KT, GCB, OM, AK, QSO, CC, PC, ADC, Earl of Chester, Duke of Cornwall, Duke of Rothesay, Earl of Carrick, Baron of Renfrew, Lord of the Isles and Prince and Great Steward of Scotland. But what do they all mean?

His Royal Highness

On 9 November 1948, five days before Prince Charles was born, King George VI declared that children of the marriage of HRH Princess Elizabeth and HRH Prince Philip should "have and at all times hold and enjoy the style, title or attribute of Royal Highness and the titular dignity of Prince or Princess prefixed to their respective Christian names in addition to any other appellations and titles and honour which may belong to them hereafter". Until then this had been restricted to the sovereign's children and to the children of the sovereign's sons, which would have excluded any children of the then Princess Elizabeth.

The Prince of Wales

The Prince of Wales is a title created for the male heir to the British throne. This usage began with Edward II, who was created Prince of Wales by his father Edward I in 1301. The Queen made Prince Charles The Prince of Wales on 26 July 1958.

Duke of Cornwall

The Prince became Duke of Cornwall automatically upon the Queen's accession on 6 February 1952. The Duchy of Cornwall – the oldest and one of the biggest landed estates in England – has existed for more than 650 years and provides an income for the male heir to the throne.

Duke of Rothesay

When the Prince of Wales is in Scotland, he is known by this title of the Scottish peerage, one that was first conferred by Robert III, King of Scots, on his son David in 1398. An act of the Scottish Parliament in 1469 confirmed its restriction to the heir apparent to the Scottish throne. Since the 1603 Union of the Crowns the title has descended alongside the Dukedom of Cornwall, and the Prince became Duke of Rothesay at the time of the Queen's accession.

Earl of Carrick and Baron of Renfrew

These two titles of the Scottish peerage were also inherited by the heir to the throne under the Scottish Parliament's 1469 act.

Earl of Chester

This earldom was created by William the Conqueror in 1067, with the intention of the Earl keeping an eye on any war-like activities by the Welsh. It reverted to the Crown in 1237, and was passed to the future Edward I. He conferred the earldom on his son, Edward II, and since then the Earldom of Chester has gone to every Prince of Wales.

Lord of the Isles

This ancient title, held by those who ruled the Western Isles as vassals of the King of Scotland, was annexed to the Crown by James V of Scotland in 1540, to be passed to his heirs.

Prince and Great Steward of Scotland

The hereditary office of Great (or High) Steward dates from the

12th century. The 1469 act confirmed that the title should go to "the first-born prince of the King of Scots forever".

Knight of the Garter

The Most Noble Order of the Garter, founded by Edward III in 1348, is the senior British order of chivalry. The Prince of Wales automatically became a KG when he became Prince of Wales in 1958, but was not installed until 17 June 1968, in a ceremony at Windsor Castle.

Knight of the Thistle (KT)

The Most Ancient and Most Noble Order of the Thistle is Scotland's highest honour and is second in precedence to the Garter. Its origins are uncertain, but its legendary status was recognised when it was revived in 1687 by James II (James VII of Scotland). The Prince is among current royal Knights and Ladies of the Thistle – under his title as Duke of Rothesay. He was installed in 1977.

Knight Grand Cross of the Order of the Bath (GCB)

The Most Honourable Order of the Bath is the premier meritorious Order of the Crown, mainly given to officers of the armed forces together with a small number of civil servants. It was founded by George I in 1725. The Prince was installed as Great Master on 28 May 1975.

Order of Merit (OM)

One of the most coveted of British distinctions. The Order is restricted to 24 members and additional foreign recipients. As with the Royal Victorian Order, the Order of Merit is in the sole gift of the sovereign. The Prince of Wales was awarded the Order of Merit on 26 June 2002.

Knight of the Order of Australia (AK)

Instituted by the Queen in 1975 on the advice of her Australian ministers. The Prince was installed in 1981.

Companion of the Queen's Service Order (QSO)

Instituted by the Queen in 1975 on the advice of her New Zealand ministers. The Prince was installed in 1983.

Order of Canada (CC)

Instituted by the Queen in 1967 on the advice of her Canadian ministers, to mark the Centenary of the Canadian Confederation. The Prince was installed as an Extraordinary Companion in 2017.

Privy Counsellor (PC)

References to a Privy Council of senior advisers to the sovereign date back to the 14th century. Nowadays, Privy Counsellors include all members of the cabinet, other senior ministers, leaders and senior members of opposition parties, Lords Justice of Appeal, and the Archbishops of Canterbury and York. Other members are also drawn from the Commonwealth.

Aide-de-Camp (ADC)

Queen Victoria instituted the appointment of a small group of personal ADCs, an honorary appointment with few duties. The Prince is one of The Queen's personal ADCs.

The Prince's coat of arms

THE PRINCE OF WALES'S HERALDIC CREST

The Prince of Wales's coat of arms has long historical links with the heraldry of his ancestors. The main shield is the Royal Arms of the United Kingdom, which has been used in this form since the reign of Queen Victoria. The top left and bottom right quarters of the shield feature the three gold lions on a red field, the symbol of the sovereigns of England. The top right quartet contains Scotland's red lion rampant on gold, the bottom left features the golden harp of Ireland on a blue field. The shield is marked with a white label to show that it is borne by the eldest son of the Sovereign during the latter's lifetime. Wales, absent from the main shield, is symbolised by a smaller shield within the larger shield, representing the shield of arms of the original native princes of Gwynedd, with quarters of gold and red with four counter-coloured lions.

This shield is surmounted by the coronet of the Heir Apparent. In heraldry this is depicted in the same way as the crown of the Sovereign except that it has one arch instead of two.

Surrounding the main shield is the blue buckled garter of the Most Noble Order of the Garter which bears in gold letters the motto: "Honi soit qui mal y pense" (Old French for "Shame upon him who thinks evil of it").

On top of the shield the royal crest, a gold lion crowned with the Prince's coronet and a white label about its neck, stands upon a larger coronet.

This in turn sits upon the Royal Helm from both sides of which flow the gold and ermine mantling of the royal family.

On either side, standing on gold scrollwork, are the royal supporters, the Lion (the national animal of England) and the Unicorn (the national animal of Scotland). Both have a white label around their necks to again signify the eldest son of the Sovereign. Beneath them in the centre is the shield of arms of the Duchy of Cornwall (15 gold coins, or Cornish "bezants", on a black background) surmounted by the Prince's coronet.

On the right is the royal badge of the Red Dragon of Wales, which also has a white label round its neck to distinguish it from that of the Sovereign. On the left is the badge of the Prince of Wales, the three ostrich feathers encircled by a gold coronet. This badge dates back to the "Black Prince", Edward, eldest son and heir apparent to

Edward III. There's an often repeated myth that the ostrich feathers come from Edward slaying King John I of Bohemia at the Battle of Crécy and plucking the ostrich feathers from the dead king's helmet. However, it's more likely that the symbolism comes from Edward's aristocratic mother, Philippa of Hainault, some of whose relatives had heraldic badges featuring ostrich feathers.

Running along the bottom of the coat of arms is a scroll bearing the motto of the Prince of Wales: "Ich dien", a contraction of the German phrase "Ich diene", which means "I serve".

Above: *The Prince of Wales with a wool carpet featuring his royal crest at a New Zealand Sheer Brilliance event, November 2012*

About the publisher

SJH GROUP

Right: *Recent SJH Group publications include Voice & Vote – Celebrating 100 Years of Votes for Women*

The SJH Group is a world-leading creative media group, delivering bespoke solutions for a global client base. Comprising five unique publishing companies – namely St James's House, Artifice Press, Black Dog Press, SJH Publishing and Cargo Media – the SJH Group embodies a wide range of specialisms that include history, autobiography, art, architecture, luxury lifestyle, global business and charitable causes.

Today's high-end publishing companies frequently serve as strategic partners for organisations that understand the power of well-connected publishers to communicate key messages for awareness and education. To this end, our world-class strategists provide companies, governments and campaigning bodies with publishing, business development and marketing expertise for entertaining, informing and engaging some of their most important audiences.

As a renowned global publisher with top-tier clients and relationships with major sales outlets, we are perfectly positioned to provide our partners with opportunities to create tangible products that tell their story, define their DNA and clearly differentiate them in the marketplace.

In a media landscape that is saturated with digital, broadcast and disposable print formats, our books command the attention and respect of readers, and provide timeless resources for decades to come. Our publications – and surrounding promotional activities – also provide our partner organisations with unique opportunities to strategically engage with journalists, clients, business partners, professionals, academics and industry bodies.

Our books are consistently well received by their intended readerships, and several of our books have appeared in the Amazon Top 100 book chart.

On average, our publishing group prints more than 300,000 books each year. This places us on the UK's top ten list for media distribution, and makes us one of the country's most influential distributors of published content across a broad range of specialist subjects.

SJH GROUP
298 Regents Park Road
London, N3 2SZ, UK
020 8371 4000

publishing@stjamess.org
www.sjhgroup.com

Richard Freed
Chief Executive
richard.freed@stjamess.org

Stephen van der Merwe
Managing Director
stephen.vdm@stjamess.org

Richard Golbourne
Sales Director
r.golbourne@stjamess.org

Ben Duffy
Communications Director
ben.duffy@stjamess.org

Stephen Mitchell
Head of Editorial
stephen.mitchell@stjamess.org

John Lewis
Deputy Editor and Senior Writer
john.lewis@stjamess.org

Aniela Gil
Senior Designer
aniela.gil@stjamess.org

WITH SPECIAL THANKS TO ...
A.E. Rodda & Son Limited
Al Habtoor Group
All Steels Trading Limited
Archaeological Paths
Ark Boulton Academy
Baxters Food Group
Ben-Gurion University of the Negev
Bidfood
British International School
  of Wrocław
Brooke: Action for Working
  Horses and Donkeys
Camira Fabrics
Canadian Nurses Association
Caribbean Maritime University
Carolyn Lo
Ceuta Group
Chilstone
Convent of Jesus and Mary
  Language College
Curteis
D1 London
Dragon School
East Winds St Lucia
Fourah Bay College, Sierra Leone
Ghana International School
Harris Tweed Hebrides
Hildon
Hornsey School for Girls
Ivana Bags
Kohinoor Jewellers
L'ecole des Petits & L'ecole
  de Battersea
Lauren Berger Collection

McDonald's Corporation
Minesoft
NOCN
Rare Breeds Survival Trust
Rebecca Kellett
Reignwood Investments UK
Samworth Brothers
Sky Ocean Ventures
St John's University of Tanzania
Tata Steel
Textile Exchange & The 2025
  Sustainable Cotton Challenge
The Woolmark Company
University College School,
  Hampstead
Walkers Shortbread

PHOTOGRAPHY
SJH Images
Getty Images

Canadian Nurses Association
- Teckles Photography Inc.

An Exmoor Pony conservation
grazing North Berwick Law,
East Lothian photographed by
Sylvia Beaumont

Harris Tweed Hebrides:
Rachel Bibby - 58°
North Photography

Textile Exchange - Tatiana Cardeal
for C&A Foundation